PRAISE FOR ASK WITHOUT FEAR FOR LIBRARIANS

"Ask Without Fear for Librarians is an excellent confidence builder. I'm eager to see libraries around the country put its strategy into practice."

Sonja Plummer Morgan
Immediate Past President
Association for Rural & Small Libraries

"Ask Without Fear for Librarians is very practical. With all of the financial pressure on libraries, municipal funding cutbacks and small, aging 'Friends' groups, libraries need to learn how to be effective at fundraising. Reading this inspired me to make three calls yesterday and today, using your advice, and the results were great!"

James Wilkins
Director of Development
Auburn Public Library

MORE COMMENTS ABOUT "ASK WITHOUT FEAR!"

"'Get REAL' will take on new meaning for board and staff members who read this book. Readable, on point, filled with memorable stories and well-tested practices, this little book is a great addition to the field of pragmatic advice to those looking for more successful engagement in fundraising."

Kay Sprinkel Grace,
Principal, Transforming Philanthropy and
author, Beyond Fundraising
San Francisco, CA

"I enjoyed Ask Without Fear! Marc has taken a subject that has been written about often and given it a new twist. Clearly, his effort is a work of passion and love. My hat is off to him."

Jerry Linzy, Senior Managing Partner
Panas, Linzy & Associates
Chicago, IL

"This short, practical book gives you a series of step-by-step methods to raise more money, faster and easier than you ever thought possible."

Brian Tracy, Author
The Psychology Of Selling

WHAT OTHERS ARE SAYING ABOUT MARC

"What I appreciate about Marc Pitman is his ability to connect the dots. I've always believed we could learn a lot from our for-profit cousins, that some creative borrowing from the marketplace could serve us well. Marc excels at taking widely acknowledged ideas from the marketplace (Seth Godin's customer evangelist opus springs to mind), and – with a bit of tweaking – making the concepts applicable to not-for-profit. Not just saying they're applicable, but showing how, turning broad models into concrete, bite-size action steps."

Joel Preston
Vice President, Major Gifts
March of Dimes
Berkeley, CA

"Marc, really appreciated your presentation Fri. I've been at this for 29 years & can spot someone like you who is both versatile and entrepreneurial!"

Preston Hadley, CFRE, President
DOMINION CAMPAIGN COUNSEL
New Hope, VA

"I've been receiving your e-zines for about a year now and they're great."

Shannon Sayer
Leadership Gifts
Harvard Law School Alumni Center
Cambridge, MA

"Hi Marc: I really like your 'Extreme Fundraising' site and read it every day via Google Reader. Thanks for your help."

Jennifer George
Director of Donor Relations
USC Libraries
Los Angeles, CA

OTHER WORKS BY MARC A. PITMAN

Ask Without Fear!

The Ask Without Fear! DVD set

The Ask Without Fear! DVD Board Retreat-in-a-box set

Fundraising Kick: A year of ask kicking ideas

The $100,000 Guide to E-mail Solicitation

The MagnetGoals Goal Setting Workbook

Creating Donor Evangelists: Moving Donors from Mere Check Writers to Raving Fans

ASK WITHOUT FEAR FOR LIBRARIANS

Helping Librarians Connect Donors with What Matters to Them Most

Marc A. Pitman,
The Fundraising Coach

Ask Without Fear for Librarians
Published by The Fundraising Coach, LLC

Cover Design by Joshua Fisher

ISBN-13: 978-1-938079-02-3 (print)
ISBN-13: 978-1-938079-03-0 (ebook)

First Standish & Wade Publishing printing - July 2020 with extensive editing by Kate Grannamann Coluccio, Ph.D.

For more information, or to purchase in bulk for your team, contact:
Standish & Wade Publishing
c/o The Concord Leadership Group LLC
2435 E. North Street, Ste 1108-171
Greenville, SC 29650
(800) 694-7430
www.FundraisingCoach.com

DEDICATION

To my wife Emily, this journey keeps getting better!

ASK WITHOUT FEAR FOR LIBRARIANS

FOREWORD

I love being a librarian; I hate asking for money.

When faced with my first large fundraising initiative (a capital campaign to renovate and expand a Carnegie library), I was overwhelmed and unsure how to channel my passion and excitement about libraries and my community into effective fundraising techniques and strategies. There was no fun in fundraising.

However, as my local municipal finance director likes to say, no money – no mission. Funds were desperately needed to convert our unattractive, outdated, and inaccessible building into a comfortable, efficient, beautiful center of learning and community. I had to get over my fear of asking for money to create the library my community needed.

When I asked Marc once why he loved being a professional fundraiser, he said that it's an honor to ask for money because you get to tell the story of the organization you represent. You get to talk about how lives are changed and communities are transformed; you stand as champion.

Marc's approach to fundraising removes the fear and provides effective ways to celebrate the accomplishments and work of an organization, helping donors understand the impact and effect of their support. His "Get R.E.A.L." system is practical, simple, and makes fundraising unintimidating.

Using Marc's framework, we were able to exceed our fundraising goal in the worst recession since the Great Depression. The things we learned from the campaign—the skills, the techniques, and the increased confidence—continue to help us successfully secure funding for the library, even after the campaign was over. We've even been able to expand our hours to be open seven days a week for the first time in the library's 116-year history!

We all know that there is a myriad of things not taught in library school. Few, if any, programs offer formal coursework on fundraising. However, the national trend of reduced funding for libraries of all types means that most libraries will, at some point, engage in raising funds to support services and resources. If library schools did offer fundraising courses, I have no doubt that *Ask Without Fear for Librarians!* would be on the required reading list.

Sarah A. Sugden, MLIS
Waterville, ME

ACKNOWLEDGEMENTS FOR THE 2020 UPDATE

This update of the text is thanks to Dr. Kate Grannemann Coluccio, director of the Carnegie Free Library of Swissvale (PA). She edited the entire book, making it far more readable. And the typesetting expertise of Goodness Okoro of gokorodesign. Thank you, Kate and Goodness!

ACKNOWLEDGEMENTS FOR THE 2012 ORIGINAL EDITION

The success of *Ask Without Fear!* has been truly humbling. It's opened doors for me around North America and even around the world. One of the most supportive people has been our local librarian and friend, Sarah Sugden. She's seen firsthand how the information in this book can help a library raise lots of money to serve its community.

She has been the biggest champion of making an *Ask Without Fear!* specifically for librarians. And she played a major role in the shaping of this text.

As in the first book, special thanks to my clients and seminar attendees, especially those from the Maine Library Association and the Northern New York Library Association. You continue to prove that the ideas here can produce incredible results.

Thanks also to the librarians that read early drafts: Sonja Plummer Morgan, Molly Larson, and Jim Wilkins. Your comments and encouragement have made this book stronger.

Of course, my wife Emily continues to deserve special mention. She inspires me, challenges me, and continues to endure me.

After 17 years of marriage, she continues to be my best friend. And my kids get special mention. They have been very supportive of my writing and speaking. Thanks guys! I'm proud to be your dad.

As always, this work has had the input of many, but any errors in it are solely mine. In fact, since I know so many readers like to find errors, I may have put a few in there just for you. ⊠

Here's to making your library fully funded!

Marc A. Pitman
National Library Week, April 2012

"Most of the people are very wonderful indeed, they almost always wish to do the right thing, and their ultimate performance, when boldly challenged and confidently led, is usually far better than we have any right to expect. Study them and treat them well, for you need them more than money."

—**Harold J. Seymour**

INTRODUCTION

I love libraries. My parents made sure my sister and I were regular users of our local libraries. Since I wrote *Ask Without Fear!*, I have been in many conversations with librarians needing help with fundraising. I've spoken at librarian conferences, served on boards, and have even volunteered to do solicitations for a capital campaign.

Libraries are incredibly important for our communities. You know that. But your potential donors don't.

Ironically, librarians tend to be awful storytellers.

I'm writing this simple guide to help you articulate your library in terms that *donors understand.* So I've reworked *Ask Without Fear!* specifically with you, a librarian, in mind.

Getting your library funded is not an observer's sport. It requires asking. Fortunately, asking for money is one of the most natural things to do. It's all about connecting your story to their story.

1. You figure out who is most likely to respond well to your story.
2. You *listen* to their story.
3. You show them points of intersection with your story.
4. You ask if they would consider investing in one of those points of intersection.
5. You thank them either way and repeat the process with the next person.

I think fundraising is one of the most exciting adventures in the world! I like to call fundraising an "extreme sport"—all the adrenaline rush of bungee jumping but no risk of falling. There's nothing quite like the rush of helping people connect their finances with their passions. It's like putting a plug into a socket: electric!

That's why I wrote this book. I want to help you neutralize your fear. I want to become your coach and help you recapture the excitement that originally brought you into library science in the first place. I'm also good at connecting with board members and volunteer solicitors. Statistically, chances are they will be with your library longer than any staff member. In many ways, they are the most important people that your library has.

Throughout this book, I will show you some of the secrets to successfully asking for money in a way that will put the "fun" back into fundraising. Instead of dreading fundraising and viewing it as a necessary evil, I will show you how you can connect not just with potential donors' check books but also with their lives. As you discover the passions and the stories at the core of your donors, you may be surprised at what you find—and that discovery may be even greater than simply funding your library's latest and greatest project.

I'm a firm believer in keeping things simple. Simplicity has a beauty of its own. Especially in fundraising. So I've distilled the process of successful fundraising to the acronym "R.E.A.L.":

- Research
- Engage
- Ask
- Love

If you've tried to follow a fundraising program before, you know it can make you feel like a human pretzel—you have to bend yourself in unnatural ways, only to find yourself getting twisted up in knots. I want to help you unwind and be yourself. I'm convinced the integrity in being yourself, linked with your passion for your library, will be the most effective way to raise lots of money and community support.

In this book, we'll also take a fun look at some of the biggest mistakes people make when fundraising, a simple way to make sure your materials connect with donors, and some assessments to help you learn to communicate more effectively with donors and colleagues. These tools will help your library's current donors and fans have concrete ways to attract new donors. All the stories I use are real, but some details have been changed to protect the people involved.

The process of fundraising for your library is exciting, especially when you're equipped to do it right. So, let's start getting equipped!

CHAPTER 1

RESEARCH

"Fundraising is the gentle art of teaching the joy of giving."

—Hank Rosso

"Donors don't give to institutions. They invest in ideas and people in whom they believe."

—G.T. Smith

"In good times and bad, we know that people give because you meet needs, not because you have needs."

—Kay Sprinkel Grace

"He who allows his day to pass by without practicing generosity and enjoying life's pleasures is like a blacksmith's bellows—he breathes but does not live."

—Sanskrit Proverb

"A library outranks any other one thing a community can do to benefit its people. It is a never failing spring in the desert. "

—Andrew Carnegie

Do you enjoy asking for money? I absolutely love it!

Being a fundraiser is like holding an electric cord and facing a wall of outlets. Some of the outlets are 3-pronged, some are 2-pronged, some are 2-pronged with a wide side, some are curved like ones used for a washer/dryer. The cord is the donor; the wall of outlets are various aspects of your library. Our job is to get to know the donor well enough to know which outlet to plug the cord into. When we plug it in by asking for the gift, *bang*! The power starts to flow!

Most people don't get to do as soul-satisfying work as librarians get to do. Many people simply have a job to pay the bills. Your ask helps them realize that what they work 40, 60, or 80 hours a week doing can actually be used to invest in something they value. When you see a donor's eyes light up, the joy that giving gives them, you'll get hooked!

The first time I asked for money as a development officer was electrifying for me. My mentor had been intending to take me on solicitations but it wasn't happening. So, I researched my first solicitation and went to do it.

A parent of a student was involved in a fatal accident the previous year while on a business trip. So my strategy was to ask the surviving parent to ask the company that had employed his wife to consider a six-figure gift to name part of our newest building in memory of her. The project was an exciting match of the donor's family interests with the organization's strategic priorities.

I went to the person's house, had a wonderful time visiting, and steered the conversation toward "the ask." It felt pretty natural. He said he would think about it. I felt elated.

Not until I returned to my office did I realize I had asked him on the anniversary of his wife's accident. Can you imagine how awful I felt? I had done research but I hadn't done *enough* research! Not surprisingly, we didn't get that gift. But fortunately, we didn't lose his relationship either. In fact, he seemed far less disturbed about the whole thing than I was. I think he was impressed by my thoughtful attempt to match his family's interests with a pre-determined need on campus.

Even with that experience, I knew I was hooked. I'd been bitten by the fundraising bug. Trying to match the donor's interests—the electric cord—and the organization's pre-established strategic priorities—the outlets—was wonderful. I knew I was possibly helping this donor make a meaningful connection to something that mattered to him.

However, talking with colleagues and clients over the years, I realize that most people aren't as eager to ask for money as I am. My work with them leads me to believe that most of this fear is fear of the unknown. This is often expressed in terms of "What if..." questions:

- What if I offend the prospect?
- What if I embarrass myself?
- What if they ask me a question I can't answer?

What if...? What if...? What if...? As a librarian, you know that imagination is good. But this use of the imagination, imagining bad possibilities, helps no one.

Most of us aren't brought up asking for money—other than from our parents—so we think we have to become someone else when we do ask. The good news is we can be ourselves and still be successful fundraisers!

To help us learn how, I tell my audiences that they need to get "R.E.A.L."—*Research*, *Engage*, *Ask* and *Love*. This simple four-step formula is designed to help you get as excited about asking for money as I am. In the rest of this chapter, we'll investigate *research*.

"Research is the process of going up alleys to see if they are blind."

—Marston Bates

"If we knew what it was we were doing, it would not be called research, would it?"

—Albert Einstein

"Action precedes funding, Planning precedes action."

—Unknown

Most people seem to be afraid of asking for money because they don't have a clue how the prospective donor will respond. Let me show you how research, doing our homework before we ask, helps conquer this fear.

Michael Wyland of Sumption & Wyland, a law firm in South Dakota, told me about a nonprofit organization asking a multi-billion dollar company to become a corporate sponsor...of a duck race. This company was a perfect prospect for the nonprofit. It made sense that they'd be willing to give. But the duck race coordinators only asked them for $250! The company did become a sponsor, but at a far lower level than they were capable of giving. The organizers had no idea what this corporation was worth! They hadn't done their homework. They could've asked for much more. But now, it'll be very hard to go to this company next year and ask for a gift of $25,000.

All of us make mistakes like this from time to time. It's just about inevitable—no matter how well you know your stuff. Many of us have a really hard time asking for more than we feel we can give. Doing some simple research will get you over that fear.

RESEARCH YOUR GOAL FIRST

I'm shocked at how many libraries don't have a good answer to the question: *how much are you trying to raise.* So many of us know that "more is better"—the more money we raise, the better we'll be able to serve our community.

But you can't structure your fundraising that way. You must decide on a firm goal. If you don't have a firm goal, start by writing out a "case statement." I like to think of a case statement as what you'd say if you were called in before a court of law (or a city council) to argue the veracity of your fundraising, your "case" for why your cause is worth an investment.

In this, you'll want to put your stats. Things like:

- What is your circulation?
- How many books do you lend to other libraries?
- What are your online lending stats?
- How many people come through your doors?
- How many access you through your website?
- How many reference questions do you answer each year (or month)?
- How many people use your computers and meeting room space?
- What kind of programs occur in your library?

- What results are your services providing for your community?
    - Social connections for seniors might increase health outcomes.
    - Online access for the underprivileged helps shorten the "digital divide."
    - Story times and other programs for kids offer great benefit to youth through the strengthening of pre-reading and reading skills; those programs also provide a support system for parents and caregivers.
    - Many libraries are entrepreneur and business centers or provide employment help.
    - Many offer support and a safe space for; homeless people when the emergency shelter is closed during the day.
    - Many librarians are *the* significant adult in a teenager's life.

Put all of this down on paper. Use stories to back up the statistics. To fundraise effectively, you must speak to both the head (stats) and the heart (emotions).

You should also get "social proof." Studies show that people are more likely to support a cause if they see proof that others like them support it. So in your case statement, get quotes from:

- patrons
- board
- members of the Friends' group
- people in between jobs using resources to get back on their feet
- employers in the community who have been surprised to find how useful the library is
- local entrepreneurs who've had affordable access to patent information through your library
- outside groups that find your space invaluable in carrying out their mission

Take pictures. I'd even recommend filming 30 second videos of people saying what they like most about your library. Be sure to tell them this will be used online and in print. Distribute permission slips for the use of the photos (especially for minors!) and collect and file the completed slips. People are often flattered to be asked. Using a good quality camera, phone or tablet will produce results that you can post online or pull still shots out for print publications.

Once you've written out a case statement, figure out how much it costs to effectively fund your library. That number should be easy. Look at your annual costs, including things like what maintenance would cost if you fixed things when they broke instead of deferring it. Don't forget to look at funding for programs and staffing.

That number may be too overwhelming to conduct a campaign around, but the research will be invaluable for your fundraising, marketing, community relations, town/city relations…even talks to service groups like Rotary.

I'd recommend narrowing that number down to a more specific project. Are you raising money for an addition? Or for more acquisitions? Or to install an elevator or air conditioning? Do you need funding for new services or programs? Once you have a specific project, pull together a case statement for that project.

Two last things to remember as you rework your case statement

1. Keep it jargon free
2. Sell benefits, not features

Keep it jargon free. Librarians are *passionate* about libraries. You go to school and get advanced degrees and are very literate. But this case isn't going to be read by other librarians. Your goal in fundraising is to involve people whose lives *don't* revolve around your library. To do that, you need to translate jargon for them. How do you know if you're using jargon?

- *Read it out loud*
  Seriously. Read the case out loud. Not skimming, murmuring reading. Print it out and read it as though you were speaking to someone. Have a pen or pencil handy to put a simple check next to areas you stumble over. Don't fix those areas right now, you'll come back and do that. Just read through and notice what might need explaining.

- *Get a non-librarian to read it*
  This is the best way to keep any of your communications jargon free. Many authors suggest writing to a middle school vocabulary. Remember, you're not trying to win any literary awards with this case. *You're trying to incite action.* To do that, you must be clear and direct. Having a person outside the library read it will help you immensely.

Sell benefits, not features. Many sales trainings talk about the difference between features and benefits. Your feature is your circulation volume, your benefit is what that means. Ok, so you have 1 million books checked out each month. A potential donor might appropriately say, "So what?" Those of us outside the library have nothing to compare that number to.

One way to translate that feature into a benefit might be comparing it to other libraries in your region, state, or province. Does checking out 15,000 books a month make you the largest circulation in the region? That is compelling.

Another, and possibly better, way to translate it is the benefit to the end-user. What difference does this high volume make in the lives of your patrons? Does having such a high circulation mean you're able to keep the most up-to-date acquisitions? Does it mean your community is stellar in reading? Or does it mean that, while your library is clearly a great asset to your community, your patrons have to wait a long time to get the book they want?

Do you see the two ways of translating this? One is to trumpet success and the impact that has on the people you serve. The other is to show how success needs more funding to be even more beneficial to your patrons. Both are effective in a case statement.

A great way to think about the features/benefits conversation was summed up by the phrase, "sell the sizzle, not the steak." Sales guru Zig Ziglar loved pointing out that millions of drills are sold each year. But no one wants a drill. They want a hole. The drill is the feature; the hole—the end result—is the benefit.

Get to work making sure your case statement has all the facts but also helps people translate what those facts mean for the library and for themselves.

FREE ONLINE TOOLS

Now that you have a specific number, it would be very tempting to divide that evenly. If you're trying to raise $100,000, it's very easy to fall into the "we-just-need-to-get-$100-from-1000-people" mindset. This makes sense mathematically, but *decades of fundraising research show that money doesn't come that way.* One of the great tools for you to use is a gift range calculator. There are a few on the web, one of them is at: www.GiftRangeCalculator.com.

For instance, to raise $100,000, most gift tables will say you'll need to have the first gift be 10%-25% of the goal, i.e.

$10,000-$25,000. The next three should add up to another 25%, maybe one at $15,000 and a couple at $7,500. Personally, I prefer to be more conservative. I'd look for the first gift to be 25% to 50% of goal.

www.GiftRangeCalculator.com

Target Amount: 100000 calculate

GIFT RANGE	# GIFTS REQ	# PROSPECTS REQ	SUBTOTAL	CUMULATIVE TOTAL	CUMULATIVE %
25000	1	5	25000	25000	25%
15000	1	5	15000	40000	40%
10000	2	10	20000	60000	60%
7500	2	10	15000	75000	75%
5000	3	15	15000	90000	90%
2500	4	20	10000	100000	100%
2000	6	30	12000	112000	112%
1000	8	40	8000	120000	120%
500	10	50	5000	125000	125%
250	12	60	3000	128000	128%
Total:	49	245		128000	

You'll notice the total adds up to over 100%. This is intentional.
(1) Costs of construction always tend to go up.
(2) Nonprofits often neglect to budget donor recognition in their plans.
Plaques and signs always add up to more than we expect.
(3) It's always better to raise more than you need.

An example of a $100,000 gift range chart from www.GiftRangeCalculator.com.

Take a look at the example chart. Can you see that you need 4-5 prospects with the ability to make that gift at each level? Using the example above, you'd need 5 prospects able to make the $25,000 gift and 15 to make the next three gifts.

Fundraising expert Jerry Linzy of Jerry Panas, Linzy & Partners told me, "Our experience demonstrates you need 3 or 4 probable donors to secure the gift. We also prefer the lead gift to be 15% to 20%, not 10%. We find today that the top 20 to 50 gifts need to represent half the goal."

This fact is worth the price of this book.

Now that you know how many names you need at each level, start filling them in. Who are five people or companies or foundations that might be able to make the first gift? Then list the next five for the next gift and continue down the chart.

If you want, you can make the gifts be boxes and form the into a gift pyramid. Not all the boxes need to be filled in by donors. Some of them can be filled in by fundraising events or by direct mail programs.

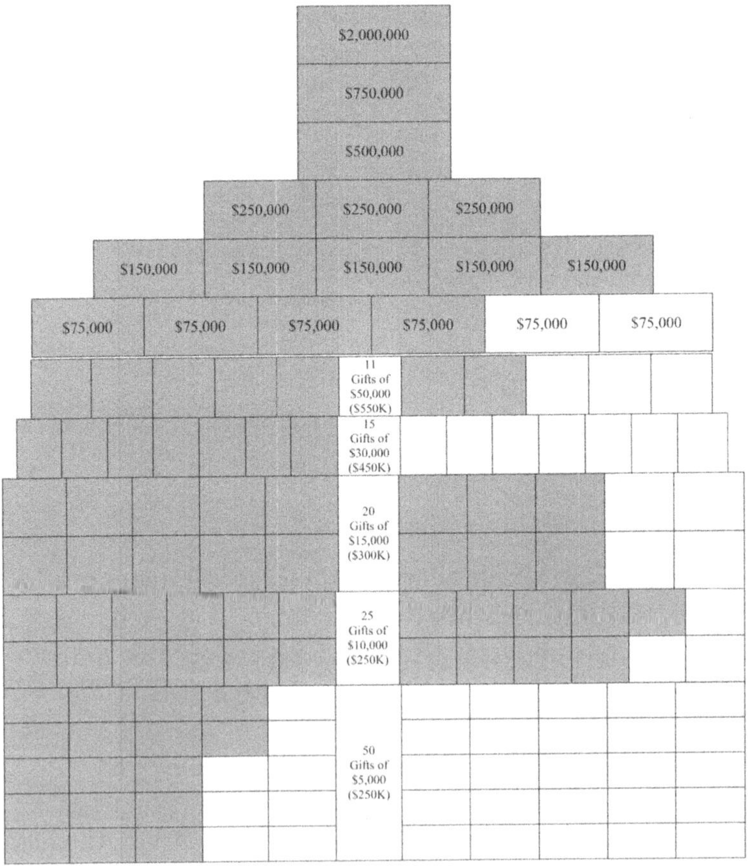

(Shaded areas reflect gifts/pledges received)

An example of a gift pyramid for a $7 million campaign.

Now that you have those names, those suspects, how do you find if they are really prospects, if they are capable of making that level of gift to your library?

One of the best tools for this kind of homework is probably one you're already using: Google. Type the name of the person you want to approach in the Google search box and see what comes up. It's pretty amazing how much public information is out there on people.

It may be helpful to put their name in quotes and spell out the state you live in to narrow the search. But you're a librarian so you probably know more about Boolean searches than I do!

What's really fun is pulling up information that is out of the ordinary. You may find a book review that a person wrote or a club that they're a part of. While those things shouldn't necessarily be mentioned during your visit, you will have a much clearer picture of the person when you meet with them.

Be careful not to rely on Google alone! A few years ago, if you typed in my name, half the sites that come up for "Marc Pitman" are for a guy who's starred in horror movies with names like "Roadkill" and "Deadbeat at Dawn." It's a riot, but it's not me! (I wonder if anyone thinks it *is* me...) So, please be sure to take your Google findings with a grain of salt.

For a treasure trove of similar online research tools, check out the University of Vermont's Research Tools Page http://www.uvm.edu/~prospect/index.html

With all the web-based tools, don't forget the good, old fashioned donor files. If your organization has a history of philanthropy, it's helpful to look at those records on a somewhat regular basis. At some places I've worked, they had file cabinets stuffed with records going back to the 1930s! You will find some fascinating information there!

OUTSOURCING RESEARCH

Another way to research is to send all your database information to a vendor that specializes in prospect research and modeling. Groups like Blackbaud's Target Analytics do this all the time. They have access to large amounts of public information, and they have formulas for knowing how to quantify that information. That information can be like gold to your organization, even on a project as simple as a mailing. By using this type of service, I cut my annual fund mailings from an entire database of 14,000 records to just mailing the 4,000 most likely to make a gift. I saved a bundle in production and postage!

PEER REVIEWS & THE CPI INDEX

One of the most effective and least expensive ways of researching prospective donors is *asking other people*. This is often known as a "peer review." People on the development committee or solicitation task force go over a list of names one by one. They talk about things like the prospect's interests, their likelihood to give to this project, and how much they should be asked for. This can work in groups as well as in one-on-one meetings.

I love these sessions because they can be highly informative and incredibly helpful in gathering anecdotal information as well as hard data. They also help you discover the links and relationships between prospective donors and other people in the community.
Admittedly not everyone is comfortable talking so frankly about their peers. So I developed the *CPI Index*. The CPI Index is a form of research that attempts to "objectify" the information. Rather than talking with each other, participants score prospective donors on three criteria:

- capacity to give,
- philanthropic nature, and
- interest in your library or the project.

Capacity: Does the person have money they can give your library? If not, he or she won't be a good fundraising prospect—no matter how nice the person may be. Face it, at some point, your nonprofit needs cash to pay the bills and accomplish its mission. Even Mother Theresa was known to say, "Without money there is no mission."

Philanthropic Nature: Is the person a giver? If he or she doesn't give gifts to other charities, chances are high the person won't give gifts to yours.

Interest: Is the person interested in your cause? Bill Gates would have high scores in capacity and philanthropy, but without an interest in your cause, he's not going to make a gift to your organization. Sorry if this comes as a shock.

To conduct a CPI Index session, prepare a list of names like before but add the three CPI columns. Then ask people to score the prospective donors in each area on a scale of 1 (being lowest) to 5 (being highest) in each of the categories. When they're done, add up the scores. You'll want to personally visit people with scores of 12 or higher and invite them to make a gift. Ask the group of peers who would be the best "door openers" to help you get in front of those people.

Prospect's Name	C (1-5)	P (1-5)	I (1-5)	Total	Notes
John Donor	4	3	4	11	Just sold his company

Don't toss out the other names! Be sure to also look at the people that scored high C's and P's but only mediocre I's. You can't change a person's capacity—no matter how much you shop at their store. And you can't change their philanthropic nature—they either are generous or they are not. But you *can* do things to get them more interested in your organization. I'd recommend beginning to cultivate these people for a future gift. You'll probably find that many of them really aren't interested in your organization or even in your cause. But you *will* find a few that will become incredibly committed to your organization if they're cultivated well. Cultivating well is the focus of our next chapter.

TWO WARNINGS

Many of my clients get very uncomfortable with the information discovered in this step. It is pretty amazing how much information is public and available. Remember, you're not the FBI. You're simply trying to help your library be an excellent steward of its limited resources. This kind of research helps significantly leverage the effectiveness of your fundraising.

Whatever you do, do not compromise your integrity. I promise you that all these forms of research are legitimate, ethical, and professional. But your integrity is worth more than any amount of funding you may raise for your library. Listen to your conscience and only go as far as you're comfortable. If you're getting uncomfortable with what you're finding, stop. Ask yourself what's making you uncomfortable.

Remember, usually the largest barriers to our fundraising are *our own* attitudes to wealth and money. Before you give up on researching, make sure you're not putting artificial limits on your ability.

Research helps you feel more secure about your ask before you get in front of the donor. Research ends up helping the donor as much as it helps you. If you found out they've written editorials against your library, you won't waste their time asking them to support it!

The second warning is: *don't get stuck on this step*. This is just the beginning. The biggest potential danger in research is "paralysis by analysis." You can do homework until the cows come home, but *nobody makes a gift until they're asked*.

I don't know how many boards I've sat on when the inevitable question arises: "Have you researched that? I know we're hemorrhaging financially, losing money hand-over-fist, but before we fix that by actually asking people for a gift, can we take a step back and do more research?" Research can be an easy way to chicken out of asking without looking like a coward. That kind of thinking will kill any fundraising effort. Sometimes, you just need to go for it and make the ask.

Now that we've established some of the advantages of research and some simple ways to do it, let's move on to our next part of getting R.E.A.L.: *engage*.

CHAPTER 2

ENGAGE

"Computer dating is fine, if you're a computer."

—Rita Mae Brown

"Relationships of trust depend on our willingness to look not only to our own interests, but also the interests of others."

—Peter Farquharson

"Don't judge each day by the harvest you reap but the seed you plant."

—Robert Louis Stevenson

"A library is not a luxury, but one of the necessities of life..."

—Henry Ward Beecher

I'm amazed by how many nonprofit folks seem to think they can just jump into asking people for money. They go from not asking at all to thinking people will just give when told to.

What if asking for a gift were like getting married? We want to get married, but we're scared to death of meeting people. So we stall as long as we can, staying inside, not going on a single date. Then our parents start getting weird, talking about wanting grandchildren. The pressure keeps building. We begin to believe we really *need* to get married! So we run out of our house, down to the nearest bar, plop down on a stool, and ask the first person we see if they'll marry us! Crazy, isn't it?

What's even crazier is that we get upset when they slap us and say "No!"

But we do that with fundraising. We need funds but we avoid asking people for money. Oh, we might hint at it or talk in general terms, but never a direct ask. At some point, our library gets into a financial crisis and we can't avoid asking people for money. So we panic and send lots of letters to as big a list of unqualified people as possible—more "suspects" than true prospects. Maybe we photocopy a sheet and insert it with the Chamber newsletter. Then we get all ticked off when nobody gives.

In both dating and fundraising, we need to get to know people before we ask them to make a commitment. We need to *engage* them in the process.

Engaging involves being genuinely interested in people, not just in their checkbook. (Or your perception of their checkbook—some folks look well off but are simply "broke at a higher level.")

- Take them out to lunch.
- Ask them about their story.
- Visit them when you're traveling in their area.

- Send them articles or email them links to articles you think might interest them.

Take note of what interests them, and what doesn't. Do them the courtesy *of trying to find something in your cause that relates to their interests.* There's no point in asking someone to make a substantial gift to a cause they don't care about!

As it is in dating, "engaging" within fundraising is a two-way process. I often let people know my interests outside of work. You would be *amazed* at how comments like this open people up. I think they start to see me as a real person, not just someone trying to reach into their wallet.

Study after study shows that people give to winning causes, not to needs! If at all possible, don't talk incessantly about your needs. I often think we in the nonprofit world look like Bill Murray's character in the movie "What About Bob?" whining to his psychiatrist, "I want. I want. I want. I need. I need. I need!" *Donors aren't motivated by that.* Let them know the cool things your library is doing. This helps them see that their gift will be well used. Show them how their gift can play a real part in your library's mission.

Engaging *is* a two-way street, so feel free to talk about your successes. A few years ago, I met with a prospective funder to see if their priorities may match with one of our events. Rather than rattling through a prepared sales pitch about the event, I spent a good portion of the time practically bragging about some innovative things our hospital was doing. (We were one of the first hospitals in the entire U.S. to voluntarily disclose its clinical outcomes on the web. We did it right on our website so healthcare consumers can make an informed decision about whether or not they should get cared for by us. That took guts!)

Letting them know how advanced our quality was also prepared the groundwork for their knowing their gift would be given to a winning cause.
The engage step is possibly even more important than researching. No one raises large amounts of money from behind a desk. As fundraising guru Si Seymour used to say, "You can't milk a cow with a letter."

Fundraising is all about relationships. So get out there and meet your prospects!

GETTING TO KNOW YOU

As you get out from behind your desk, where do you begin? It's helpful to remember why you got involved in your library. What excites *you* most about your cause? These may be the exact aspects that connect with the other person.

When you're interacting with people, start by exploring the interests of the other person. I bet someone trying to watch me during my donor visits would get annoyed by how little time I seem to devote to asking the prospective donor for a gift. Instead, I love asking questions like:

- So what do you do when you're not eating lunch at this restaurant [or whatever activity you're both doing at the time]?
- How long have you been doing that?
- Really? How did you get started?

Bob Burg's book *Endless Referrals* is filled with great questions like this. Fortunately, I love hearing people's stories. And I find people generally like telling their stories if they see you're genuinely interested. Usually people are too busy or distracted to care. When you give someone permission to tell their story, you are giving them a tremendous gift.

Another way to get to know the other person is to look around their room or office. What awards and pictures are adorning the walls? What service clubs do they appear to be involved in?

Personally, I love books so I always look at bookshelves. Once I was in a home in California that had two small elegant wooden and bronze plaques on the bookshelves. It turns out they were two patents for freeze-dried coffee! This got me excited! Beyond thinking about the potential royalties or licensing income, I started thinking about all the challenges involved in earning a patent. This must have been something he committed years of his life to. Those thoughts triggered questions that resulted in a fascinating conversation. (It turns out there were no royalties. Since he created this as an employee, the company owned all rights to the invention. Both of us commiserated about that!)

An incredibly helpful engagement tool is getting "behind the scenes." Here are some ways to engage people in the affairs of your organization that will help you when it comes time to actually ask them for money.

GETTING BEHIND THE SCENES

In his book *The Anatomy of Buzz*, Emmanuel Rosen talks about the buzz created by "behind-the-scenes" experiences. Rosen says we all love to feel like we're getting a behind-the-scenes look at something. Even if we know it's not *really* behind the scenes, we still feel special if it's an "insider's" tour.

I fondly remember Walt Disney World's "Keys to the Kingdom" tour I took in 1998. For approximately five hours, we walked "back stage" and saw all sorts of "secrets" of the kingdom. We knew that we weren't *really* seeing all the secrets but it sure felt like we were. The tour certainly exceeded my expectations. And for a person like me, that helped increase my enjoyment of the park on each subsequent visit. More importantly, I keep referring to that tour, even more than a decade later.

This is also true for our donors. This is one of the reasons international development organizations host tours of projects in the developing world. These behind-the-scenes activities help donors buy-in even more to a cause they already like.

You don't need to be doing international work to give your donors and donor prospects an inside look. Here are a few ways to possibly include your donor prospects in a behind-the-scenes activity:

- If your library is expanding, you could host a gathering at your construction site and have the general contractor or architect speak. Make sure people are wearing hard hats. There is *magic* in the power of a hard hat!
- You might hold a relaxed Q & A with your library director, Board President, etc.
- Consider giving a tour of something you don't usually showcase—rare treasures in your collection, "dungeons" or restricted stacks, or maybe even a home tour of local authors.

What I love most about the behind-the-scenes aspect of engaging is that it often can be done with little or no expense. Since it's behind-the-scenes, donor prospects don't expect it to be as glitzy or as polished as a regular event would be! The unsophisticated nature of the event actually adds to its appeal.

At one institution, I gave a "behind-the-scenes" feel to class representatives by creating a monthly one-page/two-sided newsletter called "Rep Rap." Using a simple desktop publishing program, I developed this newsletter, photocopied it, and sent the copies out as self-mailers. The desktop publishing and photocopying was specifically intended to be non-flashy and create an informal feel. I wanted class reps to feel like they were getting something hot-off-the-press so they would know they were in an inner-circle. A glossy, four-color publication wouldn't have done that.

Think of the "behind-the-scenes" possibilities with social media! As I write this, one recording artist is showcasing his week in the studio in Nashville on his Facebook page. He's including pictures, videos, and Q&A's. Or else you could tweet your way through a legislative or city council budget meeting. Or you could take quick "behind the scenes" videos and upload them to YouTube. Then they can be hosted on your webpage, blogs, and all sorts of other sites.

DON'T GET STUCK HERE

As fun as engaging is, don't get stuck in this step either. No prospect has ever made a significant gift just because you were friendly and engaging. People still need to be asked. So once you do your *research* and *engage* the prospective donor, it's time for the moment of truth: *asking for money*!

CHAPTER 3

ASK

"No one has ever become poor by giving."

—Anne Frank

"When courage, genius, and generosity hold hands, all things are possible."

—Unknown

"It is more rewarding to watch money change the world than to watch it accumulate."

—Gloria Steinem

"The greatest use of a life is to spend it on something that will outlast it."

—William James

"Much is required from those to whom much is given."

—Luke 12:48

"There are two ways of spreading light: to be the candle or the mirror that reflects it."

—Edith Wharton

"To keep a lamp burning we have to keep putting oil in it."

—Mother Theresa

"God gives, but man must open his hand."

—German Proverb

"What the world of tomorrow will be like is greatly dependent on the power of imagination in those who are learning to read today."

—Astrid Lindgren

Do you know the #1 reason people give money to nonprofits? *They are asked.* If you only could do one step of the Get R.E.A.L. process, and raising money is your goal, "ask" is the step you'd want to choose.

Which do you think is easier: Walking up to a stranger and asking her to give money to your library? Or calling a person you've gotten to know and asking them to invest in the part of your mission you know they're interested in?

Now that you've done your *research* and *engaged* the donor, asking is a breeze! The first two steps help you weed out the people who won't be interested so you can focus your asking on the people who will be.

Before you start asking anyone for their gift, be sure you've made *your* gift first. People can tell if you're committed to the library or not. You give your blood, sweat, and tears...but unfortunately, those aren't as easy to measure as money. You don't need to be making the same leadership gifts as those you're asking. But I do seriously think you should consider giving a minimum of $1000 a year—that's about $84 a month. And if you're asking a donor to consider doubling his giving, you should ask yourself to consider doubling *your* giving first.

It's so much easier to ask people to "join" you in supporting the project than it is to ask them to give money to something you're not personally investing in. Plus people intuitively know if you've given money to your library. And they are less likely to give if you haven't.

SETTING UP AN APPOINTMENT

If you're setting up an appointment for a solicitation, please be honest. I've gone into a few solicitations without letting people know I was going to ask them for money and I always felt icky. I spent my entire time with them trying to manipulate the conversation around to something that would let me make the ask. I felt like I pulled a "bait-and-switch." I'd said I just wanted to meet for coffee, but I had an ulterior motive.

So now when I'm setting up an appointment to ask for money I always make sure the donor prospect knows that I'm expecting to ask them to invest in my cause. You might say something as simple as, "I'm going to be in the area and I would love to get together with you and talk about a big project we're working on."

You could even say something as specific as, "While we're together, I'd really like to talk about your involvement in our annual campaign." Just do the courtesy of letting them know in advance. It makes your meetings so much easier. If you've developed a relationship with them this far, they know your job is to invite people to invest in your cause. They're probably waiting for you to make the ask. A solicitation isn't going to surprise them.

When setting up appointments, I like asking if their "calendar would allow" us to meet at such-and-such a time. "I'll be traveling in your area next week. Would your calendar allow us to get together Tuesday morning or Wednesday afternoon?" I find that wording makes the process of setting up an appointment less confrontational. Some would argue against using this phrasing saying it lets them off the hook because they're not taking personal responsibility for their time. But I'm not there to be their life coach. I'm there to raise money. Asking if "their calendar" will allow us to get together feels less confrontational to me.

MAKING THE ASK

Sometimes clients ask me what qualifies as an "ask." For me, getting together with a donor doesn't qualify as an ask unless I've asked for a gift of a specific dollar amount. A vague, "Would you consider supporting our library" doesn't do it. The donor has no idea what you're asking for. They may think, "I do support it. I pay my fines and taxes." Or they may end up giving $25 and think they're doing you a favor when you'd been anticipating a gift of $25,000.

You might use language like:

- Would you consider giving $xxx to our annual campaign?
- I'd like to ask you to consider giving $10,000 to o ur project.
- I was thinking about asking you to give $25,000 to the fund over the next 3 years. Is that a possibility?

I'd encourage you to ask for the total gift at this point, not breaking it down into payments. You want them to have a "deer in the headlights" look, to realize that you are asking them to prioritize giving to the library in their philanthropic giving. Telling them about payment options is great after they've considered the total gift.

The most important thing to do after you ask a specific dollar amount is to **SHUT UP!**

Make the ask and be quiet. Sales trainers say that "he who speaks first loses." It's not the same with libraries. This isn't win-lose. But think about this: you've just asked him to do something he's probably never considered doing for your library. He needs time to process. He'll be thinking about how much money is in his account, and how he'll explain this to his wife, and if this is something he can give that much to.

He'll let you know when he's done processing by being the first to speak.

Then you can tell him that $1000 a year is around $84 per month. Or whatever else you wanted to say while you were shutting up. Speaking before he does will short-circuit the important thinking process he's going through and cause him to simply say, "No."

FINDING AN OUTLET

I'm a firm believer in keeping things simple. Simplicity has a beauty of its own. Too often it's really easy to overcomplicate teaching about "making the ask." When it comes right down to it, *asking for money is simply story telling.*

1. You figure out who is most likely to respond well to your story.
2. You give those people the opportunity to tell you *their* story.
3. You show them points of intersection with their story and your story.
4. You show them how their support can impact your library and community.
5. You ask if they'd consider investing in one of those points of intersection.
6. Then you go and tell that story to the next prospect.

You'll really find that solicitations can be some of the most fun experiences of your life!

Remember my analogy of the fundraiser looking for the connection between the donor's electrical cord and the nonprofit's outlet? *Asking is inviting them to plug into your cause.* That's where the power is released! Remember the things that get them excited. If they don't care about "a hand up and not a hand out," or "literacy," or "access to computing and other resources," don't talk about those aspects of your mission, even if they're normally a big part of your prepared solicitation speech. Focus on what turns them on and ask them to invest in *that.*

When I was an alumni director for a prep school many years ago, one of the oddest alumni meetings I've had was in Boston. After tossing back a couple of martinis (him, not me), the alumnus said, "Aww [expletive]! I forgot my checkbook. You *never* see the alumni director without your checkbook!"

It was as though he had been given a script before our meeting! I honestly hadn't come to ask him for money this time. But he knew that nonprofits need philanthropic support and that relationships with donors are a kind of dance.

Given an invitation like that, and having listened to him talk about his habit of buying a $1,500 suit each quarter, I asked if he'd consider giving up his next suit and making a donation to the school instead. It didn't work but he was impressed that I was actually listening to him and asked him something related to his life.

USING PROPS

One of my major goals is to help you feel comfortable enough to consider asking people to invest in your library, especially if you're not a paid professional development officer. I know this book is helpful to them, too! But passionate volunteers are what make our libraries a special part of our community. So let's take a look at some of the different tools that will help you in this process of asking for money.

Even with the best preparation, asking for a gift can sometimes be a bit nerve-wracking. Have you ever set up a solicitation appointment and gone to the meeting only to chicken out of asking? It's happened to all of us. We leave feeling like we've really let our library and our community down. Worse, the donor leaves confused because we'd set up the appointment specifically to ask them for money but never got to that point in the conversation.

One of the best ways to help keep you from doing that is by using props. There's a wonderful power in putting a piece of paper on the desk or propping a picture on a bookcase. All of a sudden, the solicitation is no longer "you against them." Instead, you're both now focusing on the same thing. It's as though you've moved over to their side of the table and formed a brief partnership.

One of the easiest props to use is **the gift grid** you created during the research stage. (If you didn't do it then, try it now. You can create one for free by going to http://www.GiftRangeCalculator.com/.) This is one of my favorite props. With a gift grid, instead of asking for $25,000, you can simply point to that section and ask, "Would you consider giving at this level?" The prospect still has a very specific idea of what you're asking for. There's no ambiguity. Even better, they can see the entire range of gifts. He just may say, "No, not at that level. I'd like to give at this (higher) level." That has happened!

This grid can also become a great prospecting tool. Whether the person says "yes" or "no" to your solicitation, you should always ask them if there is anyone they would recommend you talk to about giving at that level. They may not be able to think of anyone, but at least you've asked. If they *do* think of someone, you've significantly decreased your research time on that new person. With permission, you can even call the new prospect and say, "I was just talking about this campaign with Joe and he suggested I show it to you, too. I'll be in your area this week. Would your calendar allow us to meet this Thursday or next Tuesday?"

Another prop that I believe just might be the most effective is **a picture of the completed project**. These are often called renderings or perspectives. Get an artist to paint a picture of what the room will look like when it's finished. If this sort of project has been completed somewhere else, get the picture of what it looks like.

Not only will the picture communicate what you're intending to do, it also shows the prospect that such a project can be completed successfully. This is significant. All of us want to know we're investing a winning cause, to a project that actually will be accomplished. A picture can help donors visualize success and reassures them that you'll see this project through to completion.

Here's a lesson from experience: If you're using architectural floor plans, highlight the existing space. A few years back, we used floor plans to help us tell the story of our expanding our nursing home. We told donors that the expansion almost doubled our floor space. But we only had floor plans that showed what the facility would look like in the future! The #1 question we got when we gave a tour was "What exists right now?"

These floor plans would've been far more impressive if the original footprint were somehow marked on them. Then they could see what the old space was and how this new space would be so much better. And they wouldn't have to take your word about the doubling of floor space; the evidence would be directly in front of them. People knew the building as it has been for the last 30 years, not how it would be for the next 30. Having the original footprint would've made it easier for them to orient themselves.

One important note: *don't use the prop as a substitute for asking.* A danger with great props is you'll succumb to the temptation of just popping them in the mail with a personal note. I call this the "Field of Dreams Fallacy" and discuss it in the chapter *7 Fundraising Faux Pas* as Fundraising Faux Pas #1. Don't give in to the temptation! Make sure to P.Y.I.T.S.—*put yourself in their shoes.* Would you make a significant gift if you received a gift grid in the mail? Probably not. *So don't risk it with your prospect. Your cause is too important.* Get on the phone, set up the solicitation appointment, and bring the prop with you. You'll be glad you did!

TANGIBILITIZE YOUR ASK

As a librarian, you probably aren't psyched about people making up new words like "tangibilitize." Sorry. (Using "psyched" probably irks some of you too!) When I give seminars, I encourage people to tangibilitize their ask. You won't find "tangibilitize" in the dictionary, but you will find it in practice all around you. Look at any piece of direct mail you receive that's trying to get you to spend money. The good ones will break down "what you'll get" for the cost of the investment. These concrete examples help make the offer tangible. Tangibilitizing is all about taking someone's abstract gift of money and making it real.

Once again, *put yourself in the shoes of the donor*. Someone's just asked you to give $1,000 to her project. They've done a wonderful job presenting their case and you're convinced they're doing incredible work. But give $1,000 from your personal account? Where will that come from?! And how would your $1,000 really help them?

Tell them. What would $1000 do for your library?

- How much more outreach could you do in the community?

- What kind of children's programs would $1000 allow you to add?
- What technology would you add? (Think creatively, especially if applying for grants. Many funders really like seeing collaboration with a local high school or arts society to video editing with teens or connecting with a senior center to get a video game system and offer bowling, trivia, and other games of interest.)
- How many books or films could you buy?

Anything. Do what you can to make it tangible. To make it something the donor can get their heart behind.

The Heifer Project tangibilitizes extraordinarily well. Go to www.heifer.org and take a look at their gift catalog.

*Need help? Have a question? Please email us at info@heifer.org or call us at **1-800-422-0474**.*

The prices in this catalog represent the complete livestock gift of a quality animal, technical assistance and training. Each purchase is symbolic and represents a contribution to the entire mission of Heifer International. Donations will be used where needed most to help struggling people.

All sorts of gift ranges are represented by different animals:

- a $500 gift is symbolized as a gift of a heifer,
- $120 a gift of a pig,
- $60 a trio of rabbits,
- $20 a gift of chickens.

A $5000 gift is "a gift of an ark"!

Every gift in the catalog describes the many ways people will be benefited. For example, chickens help Mrs. Ndagurwa

- scratch up and fertilize her vegetable garden
- give her 200+ eggs per year, adding protein to her family's diet and
- she could sell some eggs to earn income to help her market her vegetables.

Can you see how much more compelling a "gift of chickens" can be than simply asking for $20?

What I love about Heifer.org is the clear statement right under the image of the animals:

The prices in this catalog represent the complete livestock gift of a quality animal, technical assistance and training. Each purchase is symbolic and represents a contribution to the entire mission of Heifer International. Donations will be used where needed most to help struggling people.

With a statement like that, you know exactly what you're giving to and how the gift will be used.

How can you tangibilitize your library? Why not stop right now and find the answers to these questions:

- How many people will be served by a gift of $1,000?
- How many days (or hours) of programming will a gift of $5,000 fund?

- How many people will be served? How many visits will that generate to local businesses?
- How many jobs created? Students assisted?

If you're drawing a blank, check out the Online Computer Library Center's (OCLC) "Stack Up" reports. These graphically show how libraries impact communities and might help you with your solicitation. The reports are available at:
https://www.oclc.org/research/publications/2010/stackup.html

As you make your solicitation tangible, remember to not overwhelm the other person with too many options. (Refer to Chapter 5, Fundraising Faux Pas #3, the "Cheez-It Treatment.") It's important to have lots of ways to tangibilitize your ask, but use only the one or two that will best fit with the other person's interests.

WATCH YOUR PHRASING

Finally, when we're asking for money, we'd do well to take the advice of Mayor Shin in the musical "The Music Man." Mayor Shin always seems to be warning people, "Watch your phraseology!"

Each of us will at some point say the wrong words to a donor and become really embarrassed. Just read the story I call "Mrs. McTat's House of Cats" in the *Fundraising Faux Pas* chapter.

To help us increase the odds of saying the right thing, it's important to practice. I think one of the best phrases to practice is:

"I'd like to ask you to consider a gift of $25,000 to the campaign."

This phrase will be one of the most valuable tools in your fundraising tool belt. Stop for a minute and say it out loud. Could you say "$25,000" naturally? Keep practicing until it rolls off your tongue.

Since you've already made your own gift, you could easily change that phrase to be:

"Would you consider joining me in making a gift of $25,000 to the campaign?"

or

"Would you consider joining me in supporting the campaign with a gift of $25,000?"

I like to ask for the *total amount up front*. Then SHUT UP!

Sales trainers say "He who speaks first loses." I don't think it's really win lose in fundraising. But think of it this way: you need to let your ask sink in. You've just asked the donor to do something that he's never considered doing. He needs to do a lot of mental processing. He'll be thinking of questions like:

- Do I even have that amount in my bank account?
- Could I make the gift through a stock transfer?
- What will my business partners think?
- How will I explain this to my wife?

He'll let you know when he's done processing by being the first to talk. So show him the respect of giving him space. Your cause is worthy of the level of investment you asked for. It's worthy of his making it a top priority.

Once they've processed and spoken first, help them figure out how it could work. For example, a gift of $1000 is also $84/month.

Generally what they say next isn't a "yes" or a "no." It's usually an obstacle stated as an objection. I used to fear objections because I was afraid I wouldn't have all the right answers. So I hoped they simply wouldn't have any objections. But that isn't realistic. In reality, objections are good. In most cases, they are an indication from the prospect that they are interested in making a gift. *Objections are just obstacles in their way of making that gift.* So we get to work together to overcome those obstacles. Objections are actually continuing the conversation.

It's always good to be prepared with an affirming response to an objection. When you ask people for money, you're putting them on the spot. You've asked them to do something that they haven't done up to this point. You've put yourself at odds with the prospect. Everything from here on out is getting yourself back to the same side of the table.

Affirming an objection with a simple phrase like: "I can appreciate that ..." helps put both of you on the same side of the table again. You can even say "I can appreciate that..." and let the silence fill the air. Watch what happens. The other person will often fill the silence by reminding themselves why giving the gift is so important. Some people are verbal processors and just need to hear themselves explain why a gift is so important. It's hard to be quiet at times like this but it's crucial!

The great thing about the phrase "I can appreciate that" is that no matter what they say, you really can appreciate it—even if you don't agree. Chances are, if you were in their shoes, you'd feel the same way. Just saying this helps them feel less defensive.

Another effective way to overcome objections is the "Feel, Felt, Found" technique: "I know how you *feel*. I *felt* the same way. Here's what I *found...*" This is particularly helpful if you did feel the same way as the prospect.

A SIMPLE EXERCISE TO IDENTIFY OBJECTIONS *BEFORE THEY HAPPEN*

Sales guru Zig Ziglar claims that for any given sales experience, there are *generally only four or five objections.* I've worked with teams around the world and found it to be true. (Although one university team came up with around 10 objections! Over achievers!)

If that's true, why not pull your team together and have a brainstorm session? Put all the objections to making a gift to your cause—real, imagined, and off-the-wall—on sticky notes. One objection per note. Then get all the notes up on the wall. When everyone is done, start grouping the notes into similar categories: the "my kids are in college" category, the "this has been a hard year for my business" category, and so on. You'll probably find they fit into four or five areas.

Now that you know what the most common objections are, brainstorm answers. As the group works together coming up with answers to these objections, the synergy becomes infectious. Your team develops phrasing for peoples' objections and comes up with stories of people in similar situations that are giving anyway. And the best part is these phrases and stories can even be worked into both your "engage" activities and your "ask" presentations.

MORE ON OVERCOMING OBJECTIONS

Another effective method for working with objections comes from Jeffrey Fox's book *How to be a Rainmaker.*

Fox recommends turning objections into objectives. If the prospect's *objection is*, "I can't possibly give to the campaign with both of my kids in college." You can answer, "So our *objective* is to figure out how to make it so you can make the gift you want to the campaign while spreading the pledge payments to make tuition payments easy. Is that it?"

By turning the objection into an objective, you've put yourself back on the same side of the table as the other person. Now you both are working together to figure out how to help the donor make the gift. You've taken a possibly challenging problem and made solving it a team effort.

As we wrap up this section, it's really important to remember that **you don't have to answer every objection**. I was once in a solicitation with a significant community member. I'd asked him to *triple* his gift to our organization. He had more questions/objections than I'd encountered in an ask! I felt like I was on an objection treadmill. And I was losing ground.

So at one point, I asked him, "*If I am able to answer this, is this the only thing standing in the way of you making a gift?*" This was so helpful. He said actually skipped over this one and shared his biggest objection.

Still feeling stressed and a bit exasperated—his "big" question was what I thought I'd already answered a couple times during this visit!—I tried one last ditch effort. I asked, "*If I can't answer this to your satisfaction, would this stop you from making the gift?*"

As he thought about this, I really began to feel that I might have pushed him too far. But I endured the silence, letting him process. After thinking, he said, "You know, no. Even if you can't answer this in a way I understand, I still want to make the gift to help you guys."

And like that, he tripled his annual gift! You really don't have to answer every objection.

So you've asked. Chances are they'll make a gift at some level. But sometimes even with all the great work you've done, they decide not to give. That brings us to the final phase of the Get R.E.A.L. process: *love*.

CHAPTER 4

LOVE

"Be thankful for what you have; you'll end up having more. If you concentrate on what you don't have, you will never, ever have enough."

—**Oprah Winfrey**

"The deepest principle in human nature is the craving to be appreciated."

—**William James**

"Appreciation can make a day—even change a life. Your willingness to put it into words is all that is necessary."

—**Margaret Cousins**

"Silent gratitude isn't much use to anyone."

—**Gladys Browyn Stern**

"Feeling gratitude and not expressing it is like wrapping a gift and not giving it."

—**Unknown**

"The meeting of two personalities is like the contact of two chemical substances: if there is any reaction, both are transformed."

—**Carl Jung**

"Friendship is certainly the finest balm for the pangs of disappointed love."

—**Jane Austen**

"He that gives should never remember, he that receives should never forget."

—Talmud

"What is more important to a library than anything else—than everything else—is the fact that it exists."

—Archibald MacLeish

Congratulations! You've done your research; you've engaged your prospect, you've asked them for money, and you've answered their objections.

So, what do you do now?

If they say, "Yes! We are thrilled to give you a gift at the level you asked for," then you're a happy camper! (If they say "yes" too easily, try asking them to make that gift "a year for the next three years"!)

You'll want to set up a stewardship system for your library. All donors ought to get a formal gift receipt that they can use for their taxes. If you can write a personal note on those or sign them, great! (I prefer using blue pens. I've heard people respond better to blue. This may be because it looks more "real" than something run through a printer.) At some level—$50? $100? $500?—you should consider sending them a hand written thank you. At a higher level, they should get a quick "thank you" phone call. At an even higher level, you might consider inviting them to an annual "thank you" reception at the library.

One of the rules of thumb in fundraising is that we should thank people at least *seven times* before we ask them again. It's not that we stop all mailings until we are sure everyone has been thanked seven times. Nor does it mean we should send out seven "thank you" only appeals between fundraising letters.

Thanking people at least seven times means we need to retool our donor communications to come from a place of gratitude. Our newsletters, interviews in the paper and other media, and our face-to-face interactions should all be colored with gratefulness that people are making gifts that make our work possible.

Do you see how "engagement" events, can also double as "love" events? You're educating both prospects and donors on what a sound investment your library is. And if your engagement events start having gratitude, your prospects will see that other people like them are already giving to your library. That is exactly the "social proof" people are looking for, evidence that others—especially people like themselves—have already done what you're inviting them to do.

I find it helpful to think of the Get R.E.A.L. process as a circle:

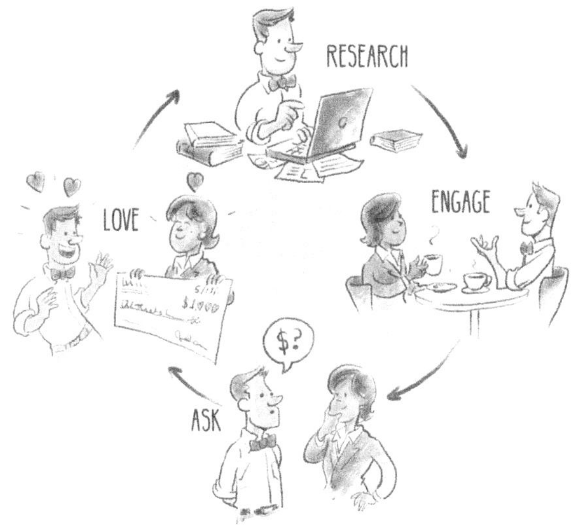

Research leads to engaging prospects. Engagement leads to making the ask. Asking leads to thanking donors which inevitably loops back around to engaging them before the next gift.

DEALING WITH A "NO"

But what if after all your hard work they say, "No"? It is very tempting to take it personally and feel rejected. Some, while not taking it too personally, will simply blow them off, flushing them from their mind. "If they're not going to play, forget it."

No! No matter how badly you feel, you can't do that to people. Your job is to develop lifelong relationships between your organization and people outside your organization, relationships that will be beneficial to both. Walking away from someone simply because they've said "no" is not an effective way to build lifelong relationships.

People are always more important than their gifts. Stop right now and repeat it to yourself until you believe it: "People are always more important than their gifts."

Besides, gracefully handling a rejection now may lead to a much larger gift later on. A "no" now is simply that...a no for now. If you've done the researching and engaging effectively, you had some concrete reasons to ask for the gift. So keep nurturing the relationship. Prove to the prospect that you're interested in him as a person. This can be as simple as sending a note every few months. There may come a point where you stop interacting with the person, their interests may change, etc., but don't just cut off contact because you feel rejected.

I knew of a donor who became so disappointed with an employee leaving that she asked for her $40,000 gift back. That was about 10% of our annual fund! I'm proud to say that the decision makers did the noble thing. Rather than threatening legal action, they sent the gift back. That kind of decision takes integrity.

They also did an incredibly brilliant thing—they convened a team of three individuals to create a strategy to bridge the donor's interest from the former employee to the entire organization. And it worked. Eighteen months after requesting her gift back, she made a pledge of half a million dollars. And she spoke very movingly at a donor event about the importance of the organization in her life.

What would have happened if the leaders had taken her to court to keep the $40,000? Or had told her there was no way in hell they would give her gift back? They may have been able to keep the $40,000, but how much would it have cost them?

Like so much of fundraising, the "love" step is a good case of common sense. This rests on knowledge that's been around for millennia. Thousands of years ago, the revered Rabbi Hillel said, "That which is hateful to you, do not do to others." And a few centuries later, another rabbi named Jesus said, "Love others as you love yourself."

Fundraising is a relationship business. It's a lot like gardening. You need to plant seeds and tend them as they grow. Just like in gardening, not all seeds grow at the same pace. Some need more time. Some are annuals, some are perennials.

I went to visit someone who had been very generous to the school in the past. A few decades before, he had given a cumulative amount equaling six figures. Since then he had sort of lost touch with us. When I got to the retirement community, I asked the receptionist to call him, not noticing the hesitation in her response. She called his wife and told me she'd be right down. As I waited, I turned toward the door. There facing me was a picture of the gentleman I was going to visit with the words "In Memory Of" and the dates of his birth and today's date. It turned out he had passed away at 2 a.m.!

I didn't make any ask that day. This was one of those sacred moments we get as fundraisers. I stayed with his widow for three hours, hearing about their life together, the trips they had recently taken, seeing her pottery kiln, listening about her kids. I was able to be with her in a way few others could have. Everyone else that called or stopped by knew them as a couple. They all felt compelled to say something but weren't sure quite what to say. Most resorted to asking about funeral details. I was simply able to be with her.

I hope you don't have something quite that drastic. But I hope you let your donors know that you care about them just as much as you care about the library. Don't become so focused on the gift that you forget the giver.

One easy way to love on your donors is to ask them how and when they'd like to be asked. And honor that as much as possible. Another is to find out how they'd like to be thanked. Many nonprofits have an annual dinner to showcase and honor their best donors. But some have asked their donors if they *like* to be honored publicly. Many generous people enjoy giving quietly, staying away from the spotlight. The most meaningful way to thank them could be by taking them out to dinner. Or involving them in a smaller reception at the executive director's house.

A WARNING

Learn to create systems that make loving on your donors and prospects habitual. Your objective is to raise money. You're not around to be the entertainment director. Successful fundraising is a constant tension between effective strategic engagement and honoring, respectful people skills. You need to focus your efforts on a carefully selected group of people *and* you need to do that while treating all the others with respect.
I'm convinced that if we'll learn to honor people more than their money, we'll find our funding challenges getting smaller.

Now that you've learned the four "Get R.E.A.L." steps, let's take a look at some of the ways *not* to ask for money.

CHAPTER 5

SEVEN FUNDRAISING FAUX PAS

"A life spent making mistakes is not only more honorable, but more useful than a life spent doing nothing."

—George Bernard Shaw

"If I had to live my life again, I'd make the same mistakes, only sooner."

—Tallulah Bankhead

"An expert is a person who has made all the mistakes that can be made in a very narrow field."

—Niels Bohr

"Mistakes are the portals of discovery."

—James Joyce

"While one person hesitates because he feels inferior, the other is busy making mistakes and becoming superior."

—Henry C. Link

"Mistakes are part of the dues one pays for a full life."

—Sophia Loren

"To avoid situations in which you might make mistakes may be the biggest mistake of all."

—Peter McWilliams

I'm convinced that one of the best ways to learn what to do is by learning what *not* to do. Now that we've seen how to ask for money well, let's take a light-hearted look at seven of the most common mistakes I see fundraisers make. I should know—I've committed most of them!

Not only are these stories instructive, they're also a lot of fun. I hope the humor will make them easier to remember *and* harder to repeat.

FUNDRAISING FAUX PAS #1: THE FIELD OF DREAMS FIASCO

During the board meeting of a client, we stumbled upon a perfect opportunity to make a planned giving ask of one of their constituents. The person had been actively involved with the organization for years. Her planned gift could endow an annual scholarship that was already being given in honor of her parents.

This opportunity was so good I was bursting with excitement! I enthusiastically explained how amazingly right a planned giving solicitation would be for this person. How such a gift might allow this prospect to do for the organization what she hadn't been able to do up until now. How the organization would benefit for decades to come from her generosity. And how her extended family may even get involved and make gifts that would grow the fund over the years.

Then I stopped to let them discuss who would set up the visit. An uncomfortable silence filled the room. They fidgeted and shuffled their papers. After what seemed like an eternity, one person hesitatingly said, "I'm not sure we should ask her *individually*...What if we just sent a letter to our entire database asking them to consider a planned gift?"

One by one, everyone in the room began to breathe again. They all looked relieved, saying things like "Yeah, let's do that!" and "Great idea!" I was completely stunned. I actually called them a bunch of chickens. (I had a good relationship with this board!)

They'd fallen for *The Field of Dreams* fiasco. In the movie *Field of Dreams*, the refrain is "if you build it, they will come." A nonprofit variation is: "if you send it, they will give." It seems that nonprofit boards really think people will make a large gift simply because they receive a mass produced letter.

Sending a solicitation letter is better than *not* sending one. But most people won't open the envelope. The vast majority of those that do will look to see if their name is on it (instead of the awful "Dear Valued Person"!) and then the P.S. Very few will actually read the letter.

Here's a shocking truth: *your organization is not the center of your donors' universe.* They don't think about it nearly as much as you do. If the case for giving to the nonprofit were so self-evident, people would already be giving more than your organization could handle.

One of the concepts I stress to my clients is P.Y.I.T.S.—Put Yourself In Their Shoes. It's so important, I've dedicated a chapter to this concept! Think about the situation above. If you received the planned giving letter they wanted to mail, would you be motivated to talk to an attorney to change your will? Of course not.

It would probably take many letters over time from an organization you love to make you go through this discomfort. That's why in the direct mail world a 1% response rate is quite good. That means if you get 1 gift for every 100 letters, the mailing was successful by direct mail standards.

Here's a tip: If you're doing a campaign or asking a donor for a big gift, resist the urge to just send a mass one-size-fits-all letter or to say "if everyone gave just $100 we'd raise the total amount." Decades of fundraising experience shows this doesn't work. Use the steps in this book, particularly the chapters on research and engagement, to successfully reach your goal. Isn't your organization worth it?

FUNDRAISING FAUX PAS #2: THE MICKEY D'S SYNDROME

When a dear friend of our family moved into senior housing, we had to get everything out of her house. But her new apartment was full long before the house was empty. With all the additional stuff on the lawn, it felt like we were starring on an episode of the TV show *Clean Sweep*.

In order to save time, I rented a dumpster. Rather than the cute little green one I envisioned, a huge construction-sized monster dumpster showed up in her yard. And it was a good thing, too! This woman was a bargain hunter *and* a pack rat. We threw out enough "seen on TV" gizmos and gadgets to fill up about half of the dumpster.

Only once did she get really upset—when I threw out a kitty litter bucket that actually contained an expensive compost starter. The thought struck me, if she hadn't spent so much money on "good deals" that she never used, she would have been able to buy bucket loads of compost starter.

This hoarding and buying things because they seem cheap are forms of "poverty thinking." Nonprofits get stuck in this poverty thinking all the time. They become so focused on stretching their money that they lose sight of quality. They will put in the cheapest cabinets in a multimillion-dollar building.

Or they will bring their major donor to McDonald's to show her how frugal they are. (Seriously. This has happened.)

Most donors, especially major donors, know that paying a little more up front will save significant amounts of money down the road. Cheap cabinets may have saved a few bucks this year but they'll be destroyed with a year of heavy use and need to be replaced. Buying a higher quality, more expensive cabinet will actually save money over time because they won't need replacing as soon.

The same idea applies when it comes to cultivating donors. Paying a little more up front can save lots of money over time. Taking a donor out to a nice restaurant is a way of showing her that we value her, that her relationship means more to us than just the money she is giving. She needs to know that we care about her and share her interests.

Here's a tip: If a donor means enough to your organization to take her out to dinner, go to a place with real silverware. Definitely show her how well you stewarded the money she gave, but don't be a cheapskate.

FUNDRAISING FAUX PAS #3: THE CHEEZ-IT TREATMENT

Have you tried to buy a box of Cheez-Its in the supermarket? I did not long ago and found the process incredibly intimidating. There are more than 10 different kinds of Cheez-Its! Some of the varieties to choose from include the following:

- Original
- Reduced Fat
- White Cheddar
- Big Cheez-Its
- Cheesy Sour Cream and Onion
- Parmesan and Garlic

- Cheddar Jack
- SpongeBob Cheez-Its
- Party Mix
- Chili Cheese
- Hot and Spicy

It took so long to look at the wall of orangish-red boxes that I almost forgot what kind I was looking for. The choice overwhelmed me enough that at first I first felt paralyzed. Then I felt stupid. How was it that I, a guy with a Master's degree, couldn't make a simple choice about a box of crackers?

Not liking to feel stupid, I left the aisle.

Oftentimes, we give our donors the Cheez-Its Treatment by overwhelming them with giving options. We're afraid this might be the only time we get in front of them. So we think that the more options we give them, the better. Instead, we are giving them so many options that we're probably confusing them.

For example, does your web page or direct mail letter give donors the options something like this:

"You can give __$1000, __ $500, __$100, __$50, __$25, __$12.50, or __any amount."

Or does it also include a check box like this:

"Please send me information on planned giving, stock transfers, creating an endowment, and corporate matching gifts."

Both are bad. Our intentions are good. But remember: P.Y.I.T.S., put yourself in their shoes. Are all these options helping motivate a donor to giving or are they paralyzing him? Options can be very helpful, but neuroscience shows that, while people like making choices, having too many options actually causes people to stop deciding. They would rather not act than act and look stupid.

Here's a tip: Try limiting giving options to three or four. Rather than sending a letter to all your donors listing giving options from $10-$10,000, why not segment donors and send slightly different reply cards with only three options: something close to what they gave last year, something bigger, and something even bigger than that. In the end, the donor may surprise you and give an amount much greater than you expected.

FUNDRAISING FAUX PAS #4: MRS. MCTAT'S HOUSE OF CATS

We have to watch what we say. In the children's book *Mrs. McTats and Her Houseful of Cats*, kids are taught the alphabet while being mesmerized by a great story about a kind lady who eventually collects 26 cats. Sharing a home with 26 cats may send shivers down your spine, but it's possible that your donors may love cats. That's why we must be careful when we speak.

Stephen Nill, founder and CEO of CharityChannel.com, wonderfully illustrates this point for us in one of his tales from the campaign trail.

I was meeting with an elderly lady, 89 years old, who had around 20 cats in her home and around her property. She was contemplating a very large gift to an organization for which I was consulting as a planned giving officer.

The conversation was going very well. Then, she asked how to go about making a planned gift. For reasons that are now lost in the fog of time, I said, "There's more than one way to skin a cat."

You don't want to know what happened next. It was ugly. Really, really ugly.

I couldn't stop laughing when I read this. How many times have we wished we could take back something we have said?

You can't assume (yes, never assume) anything. Not everyone loves cats like Mrs. McTats—and not everyone loathes the animal either.

Here's a tip: Script your key questions and answers *before* your visit. As I mentioned earlier in the book, phrases that may seem ordinary to you may not fit the situation. Be flexible and open to using different phrases. In fact, creating this kind of script actually *increases* your flexibility and frees you up to enjoy the other person more.

But isn't it somewhat reassuring that none of us wins them all?

FUNDRAISING FAUX PAS #5: THE SPELL-CHECK-WILL-CATCH-IT FAUX PAS

It's easy to rely only on spell check to catch your mistakes—until it doesn't catch one and you're wearing egg all over your face. *Spell-check is not the same as proof-reading.* Here are a couple of short stories development professionals shared with me regarding follies with spell check.

I used the word "erotic" when I meant "erratic." Luckily it wasn't in a situation where it could do any damage!

Probably the worst I can remember was in a mailing to major donors, when I learned the word public does not show up on spell check if you leave out the "l".

We've all been there, haven't we? We work on a letter. Read it over. And over. And over. Edit it again and again. Finally we mail it. Then, when we get our own copy in the mail and see mistakes like those mentioned above!

Here's a tip: We're "spoiled" proofing a letter we've written more than three times. After that, we need to get someone that hasn't even seen the letter to read it. Better still, get someone outside of your organization, someone who doesn't speak your jargon. See if they can understand the letter. If you've ever done this, isn't it embarrassing how many mistakes you've missed?

While computers are wonderful tools, they can't read your mind. Two sets of eyes are always better than one. You'll especially appreciate this when someone else catches something that you didn't see after staring at the page for hours.

FUNDRAISING FAUX PAS #6: THE YOU'RE-GOOD-ENOUGH-TO-GO-IT-ALONE BLUNDER

On a recent fundraising campaign, I fell prey to one of the classic blunders: *letting a solicitor fly solo.* (For you *Princess Bride* fans, this classic blunder comes immediately after "Never go in against a Sicilian when death is on the line.")

This particular solicitor was wonderfully gifted and incredibly connected in the community. She had been an active volunteer and fundraiser for our organization for decades. As the development person, I was paired up with her for the campaign solicitations.

When I called her to see how the calls were going and let her know I was available to go with her anytime she would like, she declined my help. She knew all the people personally and thanked me for my offer. We hung up, both feeling good about ourselves, about the campaign, and about life in general.

Then I realized the problem: *we were asking people for considerably more money than anyone had ever given our organization*. These asks were uncomfortable. And I was letting her fly into this unknown territory without me there by her side to support her. Worse yet, without an accountability person, it was far easier for her to chicken out.

I wasn't sure how to rectify this situations until she dropped by my office a few days later. I said, "I'm *so* sorry." "For what?" she asked. "For leaving you all by yourself to make these calls! I do this asking for a living but you don't." I told her I was committed to helping her make the solicitations and would clear my schedule to be with her on her calls.

She was visibly relieved. She still needed to make the calls for appointments because she had stronger relationships with our prospective donors. But I was back in as an aide and accountability person. I was also with her at the solicitations and made sure that the ask was specific and for the predetermined dollar amount.

Here's a tip: Pair up for all your asks. Doing solicitations as a pair is much more effective than going it alone. It puts everyone in the room at ease, including yourself.

FUNDRAISING FAUX PAS #7: THE HIGHWAY FALLACY

The highway fallacy comes from that ultimatum: "My way or the highway!"

In fundraising, this is when you're so committed to going in and getting a gift that you entirely ignore all the clues the donor gives. This is a way to die a quick death when you're making an ask.

If you go to a solicitation, and the donor is clearly not interested, don't keep at it. Stop. Put down your presentation materials and let them know that you can see they're distracted. Offer to come back at a more opportune time.

Who knows? Perhaps their child is in labor with their first grandchild. Or maybe a family member took a turn for the worse the night before. Whatever the case, your organization is worthy of their complete attention. And they'll probably be grateful for your consideration.

We'll get into this in much more detail in the next two chapters "P.Y.I.T.S." and "Know Your Donors." For now, remember that *not everyone is like you.* Your organization isn't the most important thing in their world.

Here's a tip: Run your ideas past a coach, colleague, or trusted friend—particularly one that sees things from a different perspective than you. Get their honest opinion, and be willing to listen to the feedback.

IN CONCLUSION

Individually, none of these faux pas will ruin your fundraising. But commit all of them and you may be lucky if you get any money!

You can avoid making major mistakes by remembering the following:

- Don't be lulled into thinking everyone understands your cause
- Don't be cheap with your major donors
- Don't overwhelm people with too many options
- Don't forget to be careful with your phrasing
- Don't fail to have someone else look over your letters
- Don't go alone on major asks
- Don't ignore the clues the donor is sending you

CHAPTER 6

PUT YOURSELF IN THEIR SHOES

"Some people think only intellect counts: knowing how to solve problems, knowing how to get by, knowing how to identify an advantage and seize it. But the functions of intellect are insufficient without courage, love, friendship, compassion and empathy."

—**Dean Koontz**

"The great gift of human beings is that we have the power of empathy."

—**Meryl Streep**

"Friendship is a living thing that lasts only as long as it is nourished with kindness, empathy and understanding."

—**Unknown**

"The most valuable things in life are not measured in monetary terms. The really important things are not houses and lands, stocks and bonds, automobiles and real state, but friendships, trust, confidence, empathy, mercy, love and faith."

—**Bertrand Russell V. Delong**

Throughout the chapters on the Get R.E.A.L. process, I repeatedly referred to "P.Y.I.T.S." Let's take a closer look at how *putting ourselves in their shoes* can make our fundraising far more effective.

I once had a colleague who wrote an end-of-the-year letter that drove home the importance of P.Y.I.T.S. He was a numbers person who wrote the letter in a way that motivated him. He'd worked for weeks on crafting this letter. The main thrust of the letter was something like:

Alumni, we need to raise more money. The parents have nearly reached their goal at 90 percent, but the alumni have only raised 20 percent of their goal. We really need your help to pull this thing together.

After a couple of us read it, we gathered up our courage, went to his office, closed the door, and told him we thought it was terrible.

As we were reading the letter, we'd put ourselves in the shoes of the people that would be receiving the letter. We thought about how we would feel if we didn't work with this nonprofit and we'd received this letter. We found ourselves thinking things like: "That's not my problem" and "I don't care what your goals are—sounds like you're not too good at setting them." A letter like this was not going to encourage us—or anyone else, for that matter—to give. Knowing how skilled this fundraiser was, I was quite surprised by my strong adverse reaction.

In an effort to help our colleague, we asked him why he was so committed to the school. We knew he had *wired* his first annual gift from Europe the year after he graduated. How many college freshman wire gifts to their school? He was now working at his alma mater. And his kids were getting ready to enroll. We asked him what motivated him and encouraged him to tell his story.

It was a pretty uncomfortable conversation. But he ended up writing an amazingly moving letter, even though it was totally out of his comfort zone. And we raised more money than we had ever raised at the end of the year. You know you've written an effective appeal when people put notes in with their checks telling you that they were crying as they read the letter. People wrote to tell us how his story reminded them this school had impacted their lives and their kids' lives and how that also moved them to give. That success all came from putting ourselves in their shoes *before* we sent the letter.

Many years ago I made a one-time gift to a large national organization. Every December after that, I received a strongly worded emotional appeal for money. Each year, the letter basically said, "We're not going to make our budget if you don't help us out now."

The first time I saw this letter, I felt bad for the organization. I didn't make a gift but I did feel bad that they weren't going to be able to continue the great work I'd invested in. But after three years of receiving these letters, I called them up and said, "If you guys are that fiscally unsound and you can't manage the money you've been given, I can't even consider giving you a gift. Please remove me from your mailing list." They were shocked at my reaction. They'd been mailing this package for years. It was their "control package"—the letter that always brought in the most gifts. It was actually sent halfway through their fiscal year so they still had plenty of fundraising time in front of them but since most of their donations came in December they sent it then.

If you have a sincere crisis, then by all means tell your donors! Bad things happen to the best causes. But don't keep warning about the dire possibility of not making budget. That's not the donors' problem; that's your problem. Crying "Wolf!" is a sure-fire way to get people to ignore you. Development isn't about meeting your needs; it's really about meeting your donor's needs. You're expected to be fiscally competent enough to balance a budget. Your job is to show them the impact their gift is making.

So, before you send out a letter or make a solicitation, take a moment to *put yourself in their shoes* by asking yourself, "How would I feel if I didn't work in the development office and I was approached in this way?"

TAKE TIME

Much of direct mail fundraising is focused on getting people to actually open the envelope. Some direct mail research seems to indicate that if you don't have a return address on the envelope people will open it because they don't want to miss out on something. One organization that practices this method crafted an entire campaign around the theme "CREDIT DENIED." The idea behind it was to share the story of a family that needed financial help and couldn't get it—their credit was denied—but thanks to donor support this organization was able to help them. The story moved everyone in the organization. "CREDIT DENIED" became their battle cry.

To keep the entire direct mail package tied to this theme, they printed the outside of the envelopes with big red letters "Credit Denied!" Unfortunately, no one thought about what it would be like to get such a letter in their mail box. When people went to their mailbox and found a letter with "CREDIT DENIED" stamped on it with no return address, they definitely opened it. But when they found out it was a fundraising appeal, they got ticked off before they even were able to read the terrific story! When a colleague shared this story with me on a CharityChannel.com listserv, there were comments from people on the list who cut the organization out of their annual giving because of that very mailing! They still remembered their shock and anger years later!

It seemed like a good idea—and it even made sense from an organizational perspective. But the tagline on the envelope scared people about their own credit so much they weren't even interested in reading an appeal. This could've easily been changed if someone in the organization had assembled a sample mailing and then asked, "How might I feel if I received this in my mailbox?"

I like to remind clients that their organization is *not* the center of their donor's universe. As board members and employees, much of our lives revolve around our cause. But our donors have lives of their own. Things that are self-evident to us are not necessarily self-evident to them.

It's easy to get so consumed with reaching our goals and coming up with catchy ideas that we don't take the time to think about what others will see when they receive our material. Just taking a few minutes to think about the people you're trying to reach, to put yourself in their shoes, can save you from myopically doing more damage than good with your appeals.

CONVERSATIONAL OR SCRIPTED?

Do you remember the #1 reason people don't give? *They're not asked.*

While I'm not exactly the biggest proponent of phonathons, they can be an effective way of asking. I've had to run them from time-to-time. If you've ever participated in a phonathon, you usually have a script when you make the calls. But those scripts can make college graduates sound like a bad Saturday Night Live skit: "Hi ... my...name is... Marc ... I'm calling on be-half of ..." Not exactly the way to impress prospective donors! Particularly if you're fundraising for a school!

The callers sound unprofessional and impersonal. Put yourself in the donor's shoes. If you're on the other end of the phone, you know if you're having a script read to you. Wouldn't you rather give to someone who is having a conversation with you?

Why not help phonathon participants sound like friends? If you're running a phonathon, I definitely would have a complete, word-for-word script. Calling can be nerve wracking and knowing exactly what is expected for each call is helpful. But I also add a section of bulleted key points so callers can quickly return to them. These can be done on the top of the script, on separate index cards, or even on posters on the walls. If they could only do three things in the call, what would you want them to do? Then put it in the bullets. (Hint: asking for a gift should be one of those three!)

COMFORTABLE IN YOUR OWN SHOES

Putting yourself in others' shoes is good. But it's also good to get comfortable in your own shoes. You have to come to grips and realize you need to ask people to give money to your cause. At some point, you have to face your own fear and insecurities.

Whether you've been involved in fund raising for 30 days or 30 years, think about the times you were afraid. Just before you make the call to set up the appointment, what is your mind picturing? Often it's picturing the worst possible outcome. "I'm probably interrupting their busy schedule." Or "I bet they hate hearing from me."

Fear is your imagination going on the dark side and thinking about all the things that could go wrong. Usually, the things you were afraid of never happened anyway. Do you remember Mark Twain's quote: "I am an old man and have known a great many troubles, but most of them never happened"? That's the way it is with fear. Many of the negative things you picture won't ever happen.

So the next time you go to pick up the phone, imagine yourself making someone's day by asking them to give and helping them invest their resources in a cause they really care about and value. This is just as "real" for your imagination as the fear pictures. And it's more true for donors. The positives far outweigh the negatives when it comes to giving people an opportunity to do something worthwhile with their money.

To help you get comfortable with what you are doing, you have to begin by asking: Why are you asking for money? This will drive you back to the "Research" step of the Get R.E.A.L. process.

Are you doing it to change a kid's life? Are you changing your community? There could be a thousand reasons why you are asking for money—and why you believe in the cause that you are leading. Focusing on the positive outcomes will help you get over your fear. You may still be a little afraid, but at least you know why you're making the ask.

And really, what is the worst that could happen? They could say "no." That's it. They're not going to lash out at you or collapse from shock. If they do say "no," they aren't rejecting you! They are just saying no to what you asked them for. And, as we discussed in the chapter on "Asking," their no is often simply a "no for now."

What if the donor immediately gives you exactly what you ask for? When I was starting out in fundraising, I heard the story of a fund raiser who asked for $1,000—and the donor immediately wrote out the check without even thinking about it. This fundraiser was so comfortable in his own shoes, and committed to his cause, that he handed the check back! He told the donor, "I'm sorry. We didn't ask for enough. We don't want to be one of your throwaway charities. We want to be on your top 10 list." The businessman was taken aback. But this earned his respect. He knew they weren't just glad-handing and that they were serious about what they did with his money.

Giving the check back may not be the wisest thing. But if you're comfortable enough with yourself, you may decide to apply what I've heard called "the YMCA technique." (I have *no* idea how it came to be called this. That's just how a trainer referred to it!) The YMCA technique is simply this: when someone easily commits to the amount you asked for, you ask, as smoothly as possible, "...a year for the next 3 years?" Suddenly, the $500 gift turned into a $1,500 gift and you don't have to go back to that person asking for money each year.

This really works! During one campaign, I'd called a donor to set up the solicitation. We'd had a nice tour of the facility and she knew the call was coming. As we agreed on the time, she told me she'd already written the check. My heart sunk. For some reason, I assumed it was for $250! I quickly regained my composure, put the smile back on my face (people can "hear" the smile over the phone!), and asked, "May I ask you a question that might be a bit impertinent?" She chuckled and said I could. "Would you consider writing that same check next November?", I asked. She chuckled again and said she would.

When we met, she handed me a check for $2500, not the $250 that I'd imagined. This was the first gift she'd ever made to our organization and that was a large gift for our first time givers. Then she told me she would write a check for the same amount next year. "I would never have thought of it," she told me, "but I will do it because you asked." She was pleased to find that a $5000 gift in our campaign merited listing on a plaque. And I was ecstatic. Having this women's name on our campaign was definitely going to help us reach other people in our community!

So as you go through the Get R.E.A.L. process of asking for money, learn to get comfortable in your own shoes. And remember to P.Y.I.T.S.—put yourself in their shoes too. If *you* wouldn't like receiving what you're about to give, chances are the other person won't either. So change your approach!

CHAPTER 7

TOOLS FOR KNOWING YOUR DONORS

"Dreams are the touchstones of our character."

—Henry David Thoreau

"We should take care not to make the intellect our god; it has of course, powerful muscles, but no personality."

—Albert Einstein

"We continue to shape our personality all our life. If we knew ourselves perfectly, we should die."

—Albert Camus

"Always keep an open mind and a compassionate heart."

—Phil Jackson

One of the biggest obstacles to overcome in any fundraising effort, particularly a long-term project, is that of knowing who your donors are. Sounds odd, doesn't it? You're probably already saying, "Hold on, Marc. I know *exactly* who my donors are, thank you very much. They're the ones that have made a gift to my project! I can print out a list of their names any time I want." I agree that is simple and important. But what can you tell me *about* your donors? What are they like? Old? Young? Wealthy? Middle-class? Male? Female? Professionals? Blue collar? Single? Married? Parents? Business executives? Entrepreneurs? Smart? Savvy? Skilled? Generous? Do they tend to be optimists? Pessimists? Do they like public recognition? Or do they prefer one-on-one appreciation?

Knowing as much as we can about the people we are inviting to care about our cause can go a long way in helping us achieve our goals—especially in our goals of building long-term relationships. In this chapter, I'll introduce you to two effective assessments that can help you interact in every step of the Get R.E.A.L. process: the D.I.S.C. test and The Highlands Ability Battery.

THE D.I.S.C. TEST

If you've never heard of the "D.I.S.C." test, you are missing out on an incredibly simple assessment tool that will help you understand people's personalities. Four quadrant personality assessments have been around for millennia. The labels range from the standard "sanguine," "phlegmatic," "melancholy," and "choleric" labels of the ancient Greeks to different kinds of cars or animals. I think its popularity is so enduring because this format is easy to grasp yet something you can use for years.

The D.I.S.C. assessment is basically a circle with two lines in it. The vertical line represents how fast or slow you process things. Write "faster" at the top of the circle and "slower" at the bottom. The horizontal line represents your preference of working with people or tasks. Write "tasks" on the left-hand side of the circle. Write "people" on the right. Each of these lines acts as a spectrum. Some people will be task oriented but not to the same extreme as others.

In your circle with the two lines, put a "D" in the upper left-hand quadrant; an "I" in the upper right-hand; an "S" in the lower right; and a "C" in the lower left. Your diagram should look like this one from the people at Personality Insights.

Image courtesy of PersonalityInsights.com

I recommend you take an official assessment by a provider like that named in the resource section. But even if you haven't, take a minute to try to place yourself on the chart.

- Do you tend to be a faster-paced person? Someone who prefers to be up front and on stage?
- Or are you someone who doesn't mind being behind the scenes, out of the limelight?
- Would you rather be with people or do you is it more important for you to accomplish tasks?

Do you have an idea where you might be? Now let's look at each quadrant individually. Remember, the lines are spectrums, some people are more like the description, some less. And people tend to be a blend of a couple letters. Now for the descriptions!

A QUICK D.I.S.C. OVERVIEW

D's are people who are upfront and on stage. They're no-nonsense doers. They get things done, no matter what. No matter who gets hurt. These folks are often what people think of as the stereotypical "leader." They're the people who say, "We're doing this *my* way."

I's are also upfront people, but they are also very people-focused. I's just love being around other people. Like a golden retriever, strangers are just friends they haven't met yet. If they have to choose between coffee with friends or working on a task alone, they'll choose coffee with a friend. They're high-energy people who say, "We're going to have fun!"

S's are also very much on the side of people, but they don't want to be up front. They're almost like Piglet from Winnie the Pooh, not timid but not needing to bounce around like Tigger. They're solid, dependable people. They want to make sure everyone's in harmony. They tend to have a great perspective on how people are feeling. We need S's because D's and I's tend to be so far out in front that they're out of touch with how people are feeling and can run roughshod over them. And, as we'll see, Cs aren't particularly wired to consider people's feelings. So S's are vital to every team. S's like to ask, "How is everyone doing?"

C's are into tasks. Really into tasks. They *love* numbers. They don't necessarily have a need or desire to be around people, especially when they're working. They study and research before coming to conclusions. They just want to make sure everything is done correctly. They'll ask tons of questions to make sure a plan will work. They're great engineers and CPAs. They're the kind of people who say, "We're going to do it the right way and *my* way is the right way."

If you're a movie buff, then here is how a few characters' personalities might fit on the D.I.S.C. wheel:

- In Disney's "The Lion King," Musafa is a high D.
- In the movie "Sister Act," Whoopie Goldberg's character, Sister Mary Calrenc, would be a high I.
- Winnie the Pooh might be a high S.
- Professor Higgins from "My Fair Lady" is a stereotypical C.

This is just a broad brush sketch. People write books on this. For our purposes, it's important to understand how people communicate and process information within each category.

D.I.S.C. AT WORK

Shortly after starting a new job, my wife and I learned that we were pregnant. Naturally, one of my wife's first assignments for me was to find out if my employer had any "paternity leave" policy. Since I had just started there, I felt extremely uncomfortable about asking. I thought about directly asking our CFO—he who oversaw the human resources function—but I decided against it. He took things very seriously, and it seemed to me, a bit negatively. I didn't want to stir anything up so I decided to send a personal just-checking-in-but-I-know-this-probably-isn't-an-option email to someone else in his office.

The *very next day*, I received a *policy statement* from the CFO himself! Not a note from the employee. Not a note from the

CFO. A *policy statement!* I was so angry and embarrassed! I hadn't even asked him. I had intentionally chosen not to ask him because I was sure I'd get a response like the one in front of me.

There was *nothing* personal in the email. There was nothing in there indicating that he knew I wasn't looking to get out of working my new job, that my query had been merely informational. There was nothing about me at all! There was just a full blown, bureaucratic, policy statement. I was beside myself!

Can you tell that I'm a high I? I took this impersonal response to mean that the CFO was questioning my integrity and thinking I was a slacker. After I'd vented to my boss and taken some time to cool off, I took my grievance to the CFO.

He had no idea he had done anything that would upset me. "I was just writing policy," he said. "Every organization needs policy to run." Of course, he was right. Every organization does need policy. But it needs people too!

If I had stepped back to see the situation in terms of D.I.S.C., I would've realized he was a high C. As such, he was more focused on policies and procedures—the task side of life—than with relating to people. In an organization, C's know that you need some level of policies to help direct relationships within the organization. I would've also realized that this person was hired specifically because the organization was full of policy gaps. It needed a high C to fix them. My question simply revealed another gap, so he quickly filled it.

To a high I like myself, his filling the gap felt more like he was playing a game of Whack-a-Mole and I was the mole! Even after our call, he was miffed by my response; amazed that anyone would get emotionally upset by a policy.

We never did see eye-to-eye on that. But we worked together so we learned to get along. Donors don't have to be that forbearing. So we need to learn to get along with them more quickly.

D.I.S.C. & FUNDRAISING

Think about D.I.S.C. in terms of your donors. Can you see that knowing *how* to relate to someone will help you in being much more effective at asking them for money? If you're a high C, you'll probably tell your organization's story based on statistics, graphs, and columns of numbers. But if your prospect is a high I, she would rather hear about how one person's life was impacted by your organization's work. This is why the Engage step of the Get R.E.A.L. process is so important. You can pick up a lot of the cues here.

I'm a high I and a high D. I guess that means I'm a 100% fast motor person! Seminar attendees tell me I talk *very* fast and usually ask me to slow down so they have a chance to catch up. I *love* people but, as a high D, completing tasks is also very important to me. One of the most frustrating fundraising visits for me was with a donor who was a high S. She spent *hours* touring me around her city. *Hours.*

All I could think of was all the other donors I could have visited. At that point in my career, my goal was to pack my schedule with as many appointments as possible. I wanted to justify my travel with lots of visits and lots of solicitations. Appointments were more about task completion than about relating to people and I wanted to complete as many as I could. That was how I could show I was making the most of my time.

As a Certified Franklin Covey Coach, I should've remembered Stephen Covey saying that with people, "Slow is fast; fast is slow." With this donor, I needed to slow down. She was investing in our relationship. She was thrilled to have a representative from my organization come and visit her and she wanted to treat me well. It turns out that taking that time with her created a relationship that produced fruit in the coming years. And we're still in touch today.

As a fundraiser, you can take an assessment to get a real perspective of your own personality. And using D.I.S.C., you can quickly identify where the donor prospect might be. If you're normally a slower speaker, you'll need to step it up with a fast-paced person just to keep your prospect from becoming bored. If you're usually faster paced, you'll definitely want to slow down for people that linger over life rather than consume it. Your fast speech may make you come across as pushy. If you're a task person, you'll need to work really hard to include people stories for your I and S prospects. But if you're an I or S asking a C or D, you'll need to get to the point and be ready to back up your stories with facts. Facts that you fortunately have in the case statement you wrote in the "Research" step of the Get R.E.A.L. process!

THE HIGHLANDS ABILITY BATTERY

Another incredibly useful tool that will give you a way to approach your donors, as well as your own life, is The Highlands Ability Battery. This assessment revolutionized my own professional growth and my marriage.

In *First Break All the Rules*, authors Marcus Buckingham and Curt Coffman explain the difference between average managers, good managers, and great managers. The book takes on the common human resource myth that you need to work on your weaknesses and be a well-rounded person to succeed. Backed by all the statistical research of the Gallup

Organization, Buckingham and Coffman show that excellent managers, don't focus on people's weaknesses. Excellent managers discover people's natural strengths and put people in positions that let those strengths flourish.

The Highlands Ability Battery helps you do just that. It is specifically designed to help identify your "hard-wired" natural abilities. Natural abilities are the things that come easily to you. Most often, the stress we feel in life comes from either operating in areas that do not come naturally to us or from abilities that aren't being used. As we arrange our lives more in line with our natural talents, we find stress practically evaporates and our work becomes filled with a renewed energy and purpose.

Through a three to four-hour test full of 19 seemingly mind-numbing work samples you have to complete within set time limits, the Highlands measures which tasks you complete quickly and which take you more time. All of us could complete all the tasks if we were given enough time. The ones that come quickly point to your hard-wiring, your natural talents.

One of the things I love most about the Highlands is that you can't skew the results. All the other personality assessments I've used ask you to rate yourself on what you perceive your behavior or attitudes to be. After you take a few, you begin to see where the questions are going and how to make the results look more as you would like. The Highlands is different. It objectively measures how well you perform on specific work samples. That's it. Either you do them in the allotted time or you don't. There's no bias to it so this method very effectively identifies your hard-wired, natural abilities.

After taking the test, you receive a very long report describing your results and how they affect your life. Then you have a two-hour, one-on-one feedback session with a coach. This coach has studied your results and is able to explain them and to see if you agree or not with them. He also helps identify patterns or "clusters" of abilities and helps you begin to strategize your life around your natural talents.

After completing the Highlands Ability Battery, my mother said, "Marc, I felt more mentally alert after spending 33 hours in labor with you than I do after taking this test! I hope it's worth it!" Fortunately, it was. After seeing the report and going over it with a knowledgeable coach, my mom was amazed. The Highlands actually helped her explain some learning styles she had noticed in herself but hadn't been able to put into words. It helped her see herself in a completely new light.

And how did it revolutionize my marriage? It gave us a common language based on an objective assessment. One of the abilities measured is *idea productivity*. Idea productivity measures how fast your faucet of ideas is flowing, not whether the ideas are good or bad. Some people are generating new ideas all the time, others generate very few. Neither is better than the other. Some roles require coming up with lots of ideas quickly. But people with high idea productivity can't always focus; all the new ideas keep distracting them.

I'm a mid-range in idea productivity; my wife is off-the-charts! The other day, she and I were talking at the kitchen table as she was eating some store-bought pudding. All of a sudden, she stopped talking in mid-sentence, staring at her empty plastic cup. Just staring at it. It was really weird. I thought I had lost her. And I was hoping I hadn't done something to offend her!

Then she sort of snapped out of it. "Sorry," she said. "Idea productivity. I just had about a hundred ideas of what I could do with this little plastic cup." Immediately the whole situation made sense and I was able to relax. That's just how she lives her life—ideas coming in a constant flow. People who have high idea productivity have hundreds of ideas thrown against the front of their brain all the time. The ideas aren't all good but the quantity can be overwhelming.

Think about this in terms of donor relations. Do you have a donor or alumnus who is always coming up with ideas on how you can do your job better? Maybe they're simply high in idea productivity. Rather than letting them grate on you, why not invite them to the next brainstorming session your staff has? Their hard-wired ability may really help improve whatever you're talking about. And if you're asking that person for money, you know you'll need to vary your approach with props, other people, and other tools just to help them stay focused.

Let's look at some of the abilities the Highlands tests on and see how these can affect your approach to fundraising.

HIGHLANDS: INTROVERT AND EXTROVERT

The only subjective part of the Highlands is the portion that evaluates whether you are an introvert or an extrovert. Knowing this can help avoid many conflicts! Introverts tend to share an idea once they've worked it over internally and arrived at their finished product. They've thought things over, they've come to a resolution, they've framed it, and they're through. Extroverts, on the other hand, start talking without knowing what the finished idea will be. They love doing the processing outside themselves and with others. Extroverts practically have to speak to think.

Guess what happens when an introvert shares an idea at a gathering of people. Extroverts in the group pounce on the idea like a cat pouncing a ball of yarn. They don't realize the introvert was sharing a completed thought, not a rough draft. From an introvert's perspective, who would be crazy enough to share an idea that hadn't been completely thought through? The idea he shared was meant to be a finished product. And now the insensitive extroverts are shredding it apart!

We've all been in this situation before. When teams learn this introvert/extrovert distinction brought out by the Highlands, extroverts start asking things like, "Is this a rough draft or a polished idea?" Introverts also get less offended when an extrovert runs with an idea because they understand that not everyone processes the same way they do.

Another difference between introverts and extroverts is what tends to stimulate them. Extroverts tend to get energy from people; introverts tend to get energy from being alone. Since people are energizing to extroverts, they prefer to be spontaneous in their interactions with people. An extrovert can be like a golden retriever, fun to have around and happy to bounce from person to person. He'll still get the "work" of the social function done without having a formal agenda for the event Whether it's talking about the annual fund or soliciting a major gift, he'll just do it in a more "free-form" style.

Introverts can be very social but they like to know where they fit or what their specific role is. Whether they verbalize it or not, they tend to want to know things like "Am I doing registration?" or "What six people am I supposed to talk to?" Having specific, well-defined roles for fundraising events helps introverts feel less drained.

This can be incredibly important when dealing with donors. For example, in one place I worked, my two superiors were more introverted. I'm off-the-chart extroverted but, unfortunately, I didn't know the full impact of these distinctions at the time. I started holding alumni cultivation events in unstructured environments like brew pubs. These fit my personality so I thought they must be good for everyone, especially because the alumni seemed to have a blast.

I was shocked to find that both of my superiors found these events *very* draining. Knowing what I know now, I should have given them an outline of the event's purpose, a list of the expected participants, and what role I'd have liked them to play. These were great with people and gifted fundraisers, but in a manner that's different from mine. I should have also mixed these informal events with more formal ones, like a sit down dinner. My guess is that we would have more effectively served the alumni too. I bet more introverted folks didn't come to the brew pubs for the same reasons my supervisors stopped going!

HIGHLANDS: GENERALIST AND SPECIALIST

According to the research done by the Highland Company, about 75% of the population is composed of "generalists"; the remaining 25% are "specialists." When you ask a *generalist* what they do, they tend to tell you in terms of what their organization does, "Well, we help feed kids in central Africa." A *specialist* answering the same question will say, "I make sure that donors are cultivated appropriately and stewarded well." They describe their personal specific duties, not the overall team goals.

A generalist is like a casserole—all the ingredients are blended together to form an end product. Most of the specific ingredients are not distinguishable in the final product. A specialist is like a Waldorf salad. All the ingredients are separately definable—the lettuce, the walnuts, the apple slices, etc. And each of these separate elements make a distinct end product without losing their distinctiveness.

If generalists are a mile wide and an inch deep, specialists are an inch wide and a mile deep. So if you've asked the donor prospect, "What do you do?" and they answer in terms of their specific duties, you know you're probably talking to a specialist. They may not know about a lot of things, but what they know they know *very* well. So focus the conversation on areas that will let the specialist showcase their individualized knowledge. Specialists *love* showing off what they know. (As a specialist myself, that's probably why I've written this book!)

Knowing whether your prospect is a generalist or a specialist can also help you determine how much detail to give about your organization. Specialists will probably prefer to get to know one aspect of your organization in great detail. Generalists will tend to be inspired by a broad overview. This in turn will help you create the most effective solicitation strategy. Specialists will probably prefer to be very specific and strategic in their gifts, generalists will probably be more comfortable with fewer restrictions. And in thinking about how to thank donors, specialists might prefer being highlighted as individuals where generalists might be pleased to be seen as part of an important team.

HIGHLANDS: CLASSIFICATION AND CONCEPT ORGANIZATION

Two more talents identified by the Highlands are *classification* and *concept organization*. High *classification* people are those who tend to love chaos and flying by the seat of their pants. They can walk into a situation and immediately spot the problems. Low classification people on the other hand tend to need some more structure. They need to do some analysis before pointing out where the problems may be.

People high in *concept organization* are able to organize everything in their head. People lower in concept organization tend to rely on planners and filing cabinets. They need lots of props to help them organize their concepts. Both classification and concept organization are crucial in asking for money.

If you're high in *classification*, you can almost instantly zoom in on what's important when talking with a potential donor. You don't really know how to do it, you just do. But if you're not high in classification, you won't be as good at winging it. You should create a process to work in order to ease into the solicitation and find out what the person's hot buttons are. (I've tried to leave my Get R.E.A.L. process open enough for high classification types but structured enough for those wanting a system.)

The higher you are in *concept organization*, the easier it is for you to make things quickly understandable to others. People will ask you a question and you find it easy to explain even difficult concepts. The lower you are in concept organization, the more time and effort such an explanation will take. You'll still be very successful at fundraising. But you'll probably take much more time preparing your story before going into a solicitation. You may need pictures of the people you're helping or pictures of the buildings you want to construct in order to begin the process.

This knowledge can also come in handy when you are making solicitations. For example, if your prospect is high in classification, you'll need to be able to move through your presentation quickly. They will rapidly grasp the ideas you're presenting and be ready to move on to the next point, often before you are. Don't bore them, keep moving. You're not trying to convert them to your cause, you're trying to move them to making a gift. Conversion can happen later. For now, keep them interested.

On the other hand, if you're too fast with a person lower in classification, you'll risk sounding like a con artist. That's never an effective way to ethically raise money! So slow down a bit. Take a bit more time explaining things. Sure, you want to ask for a gift. But you also would like to form a life-long relationship between your donor and your nonprofit.

What if your potential donor is low in concept organization? Again, having props and pictures like those discussed in the "Ask" step of the Get R.E.A.L. process will be really helpful, even if you don't personally need them. Having an outline that you're working through, a step-by-step process of making the case and leading to the ask might be good. But if your prospect is really good at explaining things, they're probably higher in concept organization, so you'll want to stick less rigidly to your outline.

HIGHLANDS: VERBAL AND TONAL MEMORY

We could go through all 19 abilities, but we won't For the last set, let's look at *verbal memory* and *tonal memory*. The Highlands defines *verbal memory* as the ability to take in written information. If you're low in verbal memory, reading something isn't the best way for you to remember the information. *Tonal memory* is defined as your ability to take in information by listening to it. People high in tonal memory can hear a lecture or audio book and easily remember the content for months or years.

If you're high in tonal memory, you can take in information without taking notes. My sister is so high in tonal memory, she used to knit in her college physics classes! She said the knitting helped her focus and listen better than note taking did!

Letters and brochures are great for people high in verbal memory. They read them and remember what they've read. But what about your donors high in tonal memory? Your well-crafted letters just don't work for them. Perhaps coming to an in-person event with speakers would be a better fit. Or maybe it would be good to augment your mailings with a periodic audio recording (CD or podcast) from your CEO. Or even a quick video recording posted on your site and emailed to them.

We've only looked at a few of the more than 15 talents the Highlands identifies. By now you may be asking yourself, "*This* was supposed to make it *easier* for me to ask for money?!" I firmly believe it will. Although we like to think we're all the same, we have quite distinct differences. As fundraisers, it's important for us to pay attention to these differences. With the R.E.A.L. process, you've got the tools you need already to be an effective fundraiser, even without the content in this chapter. But knowing about D.I.S.C. and natural abilities will help you become incredibly effective, both in asking for money *and* in growing long-term relationships with people that love your organization!

CHAPTER 8

SUMMARY

"You give little when you give of your possessions. It is when you give of yourself that you truly give."

—Kahil Gibran

"The price of living is giving."

—Unknown

"It is only in the giving of oneself to others that we truly live."

—Ethel Percy Andrus

"Sacrifice is giving up something good for something better."

—Unknown

"Real generosity to the future lies in giving all to the present."

—**Albert Camus**

"In the long run, we get no more than we have been willing to risk giving."

—**Sheldom Kopp**

"The best thing about giving of ourselves is that what we get is always better than what we give. The reaction is greater than the action."

—**Orison Swett Marden**

"The real test of success is whether a life has been a happy one and a happy giving one."

—**Sir Henry Newbolt**

"Remember the words of the Lord Jesus, how he said, it is more blessed to give than to receive."

—**Acts 20:35**

"We make a living by what we get, but we make a life by what we give."

—Winston Churchill

"Life is an echo—what you send out comes back."

—Unknown

"There is a wonderful mythical law of nature that the three things we crave most in life—happiness, freedom, and peace of mind—are always attained by giving them to someone else."

—Peyton Conway March

"Complete possession is proved only by giving. All you are unable to give possesses you."

—Andre Gide

"No person was ever honored for what he received. Honor has been the reward for what he gave."

—Calvin Coolidge

"Giving opens the way for receiving."

—Florence Scovel Shinn

"I have found that among its other benefits, giving liberates the soul of the giver."

—Maya Angelou

"We ourselves feel that what we are doing is just a drop in the ocean. But the ocean would be less because of that missing drop."

—Mother Teresa

"A generous man will prosper; he who refreshes others will be refreshed."

—Proverbs 11:25

"Apart from the ballot box, philanthropy presents the one opportunity the individual has to express his meaningful choice over the direction in which our society will progress."

—George G. Kirstein

Congratulations! You've reached the end of the book! Whether you're a committed volunteer or a paid staff member, you're much more equipped to go out and fund your library.

You've learned detailed ways to go about the Get R.E.A.L. process: Research, Engage, Ask, and Love. You've explored the seven biggest mistakes we make when trying to raise money. You've learned how putting yourself in the donor's shoes can make your fundraising exponentially more successful. And you've been introduced to a couple of great tools to help you relate with other people more effectively and ask them to support your nonprofit in an approach that's tailored to them.

That's it. You're finished the book. But you're only just beginning your journey.

One of my favorite quotes from Glenn Bland's classic book *Success, the Glenn Bland Method* is:
"Shoot for the moon and if you miss, you can hit the eagle. Shoot for the eagle and miss, you'll hit the ground."

Setting high goals is an important thing. With a nonprofit, you don't necessarily want to trumpet the highest goals. Nothing is more debilitating than announcing that you fell way short of your goals. But, we must get over our fear of what might happen and be tenacious in going after big gifts. If we don't ask, we'll never know.

Use the R.E.A.L. steps. Better yet, try teaching them to someone you collaborate with. You'll remember them much better if you try to teach these four steps to someone this week.

Please drop me a line if I can be of assistance. My email is marc@fundraisingcoach.com.

APPENDIX

TOOLS PAGE

RESEARCH

- Google.com
- Blackbaud Analytics http://www.blackbaud.com/
- WeatlhEngine.com http://wealthengine.com/
- DonorSearch.com http://donorsearch.com/
- GiftRangeCalculator.com http://www.GiftRangeCalculator.com/
- Sumac's Gift Range Calculator https://www.sumac.com/fundraising-gift-range-calculator/

ENGAGE

- *The Millionaire Next Door* by Thomas Stanley and William Danko (2010) https://amzn.to/2CuUanv
- *Endless Referrals* by Bob Burg http://amzn.to/NFop3Q

- *The Anatomy of Buzz* by Emmanuel Rosen
  http://amzn.to/M99JfH
- *Creating Customer Evangelists* by Jackie Huba and Ben McConnell
  http://amzn.to/KWUfcj
- *Who's Telling YOUR Story?* by Marc A. Pitman
  http://amzn.to/LstDGl

ASK

- *Asking* by Jerry Panas
  http://amzn.to/Ph6dnk
- *50 Asks in 50 Days* by Amy Eisenstein
  http://amzn.to/Ox4CIR
- AskingMatters.com Asking Style Profile
  http://www.askingmatters.com/find-your-asking-style/
- *The Ask Without Fear! DVD series*
  http://www.FundraisingCoachDVDs.com/
- The Self-Guided Ask Without Fear Full Day Retreat
  http://www.BoardRetreatPacks.com/
- Board Retreat Party Pack
  https://fundraisingcoach.com/board-retreat-party-pack/

LOVE

- *How to Win Friends and Influence People* by Dale Carnegie
  http://amzn.to/LSgYdK
- *Growing Givers' Hearts* by Thomas Jeavons and Rebekah Burch Basinger
  http://amzn.to/RnT7Dh
- *Love is the Killer App* by Tim Sanders
  http://amzn.to/Ph8FKH

OTHER

- *Life is Tremendous* by Charlie "Tremendous" Jones
  http://amzn.to/M8byrM
- *Success: The Glenn Bland Method* by Glenn Bland
  http://amzn.to/KWWpsn
- *Movie Mondays:* free weekly videos to help you with your fundraising
  http://MovieMondaysVideos.com/
- Highlands Ability Battery
  https://www.highlandsco.com/
- DISC
  http://www.personality-insights.com/

ABOUT THE AUTHOR

Internationally acclaimed speaker and fundraising coach Marc A. Pitman is the founder of The Concord Leadership Group which includes FundraisingCoach.com and TheNonprofitAcademy.com. He loves asking people for money and is often heard saying, "Fundraising is an extreme sport!"

A recognized thought leader, Marc has appeared in publications around the world. His leadership coaching and fundraising expertise has been seen on TV stations like NBC, Al Jazeera, and Fox News and on radio programs on CBS, WGN, and the Canadian Broadcasting Corporation. His energetic and engaging keynotes and trainings have brought him to conferences and nonprofits all over the world, including The Netherlands, Sweden, New Zealand, Mexico, and Bermuda.

His FundraisingCoach.com blog is read by thousands of people around the world each month and is recognized by The Atlantic as "1 of 5 Philanthropic Blogs Fundraisers *Need* to Read." His clients call him "The Johnny Appleseed of Fundraising" and an "approachable expert" that helps them reconnect with the passion that got them into fundraising in the first place.

That passion has inspired people to translate his book *Ask Without Fear!* into Polish, Dutch, Chinese, and Spanish.

When he's not helping others get passionate about raising money, he enjoys coffee, home brewing, reading, and travel. And if you pass him in his car, he'll probably be singing 80's tunes loud enough to embarrass his family.

To sign up for his free blog and other free resources, go to both http://FundraisingCoach.com/ and http://TheNonprofitAcademy.com/.

To learn more about having Marc speak to your team or conference, go to: http://FundraisingCoach.com/Speaker/

TO ORDER MORE COPIES OR TO BOOK MARC TO SPEAK AT YOUR NEXT EVENT:

Phone: (317) 296-7886

Mail: Standish & Wade Publishing
2435 E North St, Ste 1108-171
Greenville, SC 29615

E-mail: marc@fundraisingcoach.com

Website: www.FundraisingCoach.com

Twitter: http://twitter.com/marcapitman

For the DVD companion to *Ask Without Fear!* go to:
www.FundraisingCoachDVDs.com

BOARD RETREAT Party PACK

INCLUDES:

1 - "Ask Without Fear" DVD - Includes the get R.E.A.L. training videos
1 - "Ask Without Fear" Resource CD
5 - Board Retreat plan, checklist, and instructional sheets
10 - "Ask Without Fear" Books

Made in the USA
Monee, IL
18 March 2026

46281835R00069